World War II for Kids

A History with 21 Activities

Richard Panchyk

CHICAGO
REVIEW
PRESS

For Mimi, Opi, and Bela

The stories of their courage and strength give me inspiration.

COVER DESIGN: Joan Sommers Design, Chicago
INTERIOR DESIGN: Monica Baziuk
INTERIOR ILLUSTRATION: Mark Baziuk
PHOTO CREDITS
Front Cover Images: Portraits left to right: Stalin, Roosevelt, Hitler, Mussolini, Churchill, and Hirohito (Roosevelt, Stalin, Churchill courtesy of Library of Congress, Prints and Photographs Division, LC-US262-32833; Mussolini and Hirohito, © Corbis); "Save Rubber" poster courtesy of Library of Congress, Prints and Photographs Division, WPA Poster Collection, LC-USZC2-920; Hitler youth, © Bettmann/Corbis; "We Can Do It!" poster, J. Howard Miller, c. 1942, © Corbis.
Back Cover Images: Pilot courtesy of Howard Scott; Iwo Jima courtesy of National Archives.
All other cover images courtesy of the author.
Interior Images:
pages xii, 1, 3, 19, 20, 23, 46, 56, 89, 97, 110, 132 courtesy of Franklin Delano Roosevelt Library
page 25 courtesy of Elina Leonova
pages 37, 111, 119, 140, 141 courtesy of National Archives
page 49 courtesy of Peter Prommersberger
page 64 copyright © 2002 by Universal Studios. Courtesy of Universal Studios Publishing Rights, a Division of Universal Studios Licensing, Inc. All rights reserved.
pages 70, 78 courtesy of Howard Scott
page 101 courtesy of Eva Arvai
pages 102, 107 photos by IPW Team #10, Second Cavalry, under command of Ferdinand Sperl
page 108 photo by Bill Harvay
page 117 courtesy of Anita Weisbord
pages 124, 131 courtesy of Frigyes Gellert
All other photos by the author or from the author's collection.

Library of Congress Cataloging-in-Publication Data

Panchyk, Richard.
    World War II for kids : a history with 21 activities / Richard Panchyk.
        p. cm.
    Summary: Describes the causes and history of World War II, and includes interviews with participants and suggested activities.
    Includes bibliographical references and index.
    ISBN 1-55652-455-2
    1. World War, 1939–1945—Campaigns, Europe—Juvenile literature.
2. World War, 1939–1945—Campaigns, Pacific Area—Juvenile literature.
[1. World War, 1939–1945.] I. Title: World War 2 for kids. II. Title: World War two for kids. III. Title.
D743.7.P36 2002
940.53—dc21   2002155462

Published by Chicago Review Press, Incorporated
814 North Franklin Street
Chicago, Illinois 60610
ISBN-13: 978-1-55652-455-4
ISBN-10: 1-55652-455-2
Printed in China
10 9 8

CONTENTS

THIS BOOK IS
STANDARD LENGTH,
COMPLETE AND UNABRIDGED,
MANUFACTURED UNDER WARTIME CONDITIONS
IN CONFORMITY WITH ALL GOVERNMENT
REGULATIONS CONTROLLING THE USE
OF PAPER AND OTHER MATERIALS

ACKNOWLEDGMENTS

A very special thanks to former President Clinton, Senator John McCain, and Senator Ernest Hollings for taking the time to share their thoughts about World War II.

A special thanks to Eva Arvai, who served as a contact point, interviewer, and translator and spent many hours dedicated to the book. Thanks to Elina Leonova for her excellent Russian translations and for conducting, arranging, and translating interviews on my behalf. Thanks to Axel Uhrig for his German translation efforts and for conducting an interview on my behalf. Big thanks to Barbara Osgood and Helga Schnitger for their German translation efforts. Thanks to John Vetter for moral support, for reviewing the manuscript, and for very useful assistance on the military aspects of warfare. Thanks to Gary Jansen for providing some useful books. Thanks to Howard Scott for his considerable help and encouragement. Thanks to Amy Harrison for her help in contacting some of the people interviewed in this book. Thanks to Patrick Kelly for reviewing part of the manuscript. Thanks to Robert Panchyk for information on firearms. Thanks to Lou Holtz for his help. Thanks to Anatoly Lednyak for his help.

A heartfelt thanks to all those who gave their time and memories to this project, and helped make this book better: Eva Arvai, Chris Costello, Asya Dinershtyn, George Dunn, Frigyes Gellert, Ruth Harley, Clare Harvay, Willy Heilmann, Musya Leonova, Laszlo Marczali, William McLean, Mildred Montag, Magda Pollai, Jean Prommersberger, Peter Prommersberger, Joan Quinn, George Scott, Howard Scott, Helga Schnitger, Ferdinand Sperl, George Treusch, Tibor Vadasz, Anita Weisbord, Agnes Wieschenberg, Peter Wieschenberg, Tony Yoshizawa.

Thanks also to those who were interviewed or had written down their memories previously and have since passed away, especially Bill Harvay and Mario Salvadori. Of course, thanks to those who contributed their memories but did not wish to be named, especially "Claudette." Thanks to those whose excerpted letters help give the book an even more personal feel.

Thanks also to my wife, Caren, for extensive use of her editorial and indexing skills, and to Caren, Matthew, and Elizabeth for their patience and encouragement. And last but not least, thanks to my editors, Cynthia Sherry and Jerome Pohlen, for seeing this project through to its fruition.

FOREWORD

> My father and grandfather, both combat commanders in World War II, were my first heroes. Young Americans today may not enjoy the privilege afforded an old man of such direct ties to war's eyewitnesses, which makes the role of books like this one all the more important. It is my hope that the history of World War II, rendered accessible to younger students in Richard Panchyk's readable account, will inspire another generation of Americans as we wage a new struggle against the enemies of freedom.

John McCain

John S. McCain
United States Senator

➤ Vice Admiral John S. McCain (left) and Adm. William F. Halsey, Commander, 3rd Flt., hold a conference on board USS *New Jersey* enroute to the Philippines.

Senator McCain served in the U.S. Navy from 1958 to 1981, before being elected to Congress in 1982. His father, Admiral John S. McCain, Jr. (1911–1981), was a submarine commander in the Pacific. His grandfather, Admiral John S. McCain (1884–1945), commanded the highly successful Aircraft Carrier Task Force 38 in the Pacific and was present for the surrender of the Japanese on September 2, 1945, aboard the USS Missouri.

LETTER FROM PRESIDENT CLINTON

WILLIAM JEFFERSON CLINTON

March 16, 2001

Dear Richard:

Thank you for asking for my thoughts on the importance of teaching World War II history to our children.

World War II was the turning point of the 20th Century. If we seek to understand the war -- from its origins to its far-reaching consequences -- we can gain crucial insight into the world we know today. In studying World War II, we honor the legacy of the 16 million Americans who fought in the global struggle against tyranny and the millions of our countrymen whose determination and dedication on the home front made possible our military victories overseas.

Best wishes for continued success.

Sincerely,

Bill Clinton

William Jefferson Clinton was the forty-second president (1993–2001). President Clinton, the first American president to be born after World War II, signed legislation in 1993 authorizing the construction of a memorial to those who served their country in World War II. On Veterans Day 1995, he dedicated the site of the World War II Memorial in Washington, D.C., and on Veterans Day 2000, he took part in the groundbreaking ceremonies.

INTRODUCTION

Recent history is so fascinating because you can still touch it. You can still meet and talk to people who were there when the events of World War II took place. It is up to us to take advantage of these eyewitnesses to history before it is too late. Hearing the stories from survivors helps the words leap off the page and make history real.

When you read this book, you will find interviews and stories from all kinds of people about their experiences during World War II. You will learn how to interview people yourself and record their words for your children and grandchildren. Now is the time to preserve the events that your parents, aunts, uncles, grandparents, and neighbors witnessed. You will be surprised what you discover.

I have made every effort to include as much firsthand information as possible in this book. There are three ways I have used this information.

The first way uses excerpts from actual letters written by soldiers or civilians between 1939 and 1945. These letters help give us an idea what people were thinking during the war.

The second way quotes people's memories of the war word for word. I have not added anything except to clarify a word here and there. Anything I have added appears in brackets [ ]. These quotes appear as sidebars.

The third way adds facts and information from other sources to various individuals' personal stories. Sometimes I found that a person had an interesting story to tell, but it needed to be put into context with other events and facts. In this case the story is not a direct quote, but may include direct quotes within the text. Some of these stories appear as sidebars, but a few are included as part of the main text of the book.

Memories, especially those from 60 long years ago, are not always completely accurate. Sometimes memories contain both facts and opinions. It is up to you to separate facts from opinions and get a feeling for what life was like for each of the people whose stories appear in this book.

As you read this book you will realize that each of the millions of people who lived through the war had a different experience. Some fought on the battlefield and some fought on the home front. Some were safe and some nearly died. The war raged on in dozens of countries around the world, across thousands of miles and spanning vast oceans. It is impossible to sum up the war in one short book, but I have done my best.

Always remember that wars are fought by real people—as real as your sisters and brothers, aunts and uncles, parents and grandparents. In fact, no matter where your family members were between 1939 and 1945, their lives were in some way affected by World War II.

As President Clinton wrote in his introductory letter, World War II was the turning point of the 20th century. Our lifestyle and our very existence today hinge on the events and outcome of World War II.

This is a history book, but it is also the story of all of us.

MAP OF EUROPE

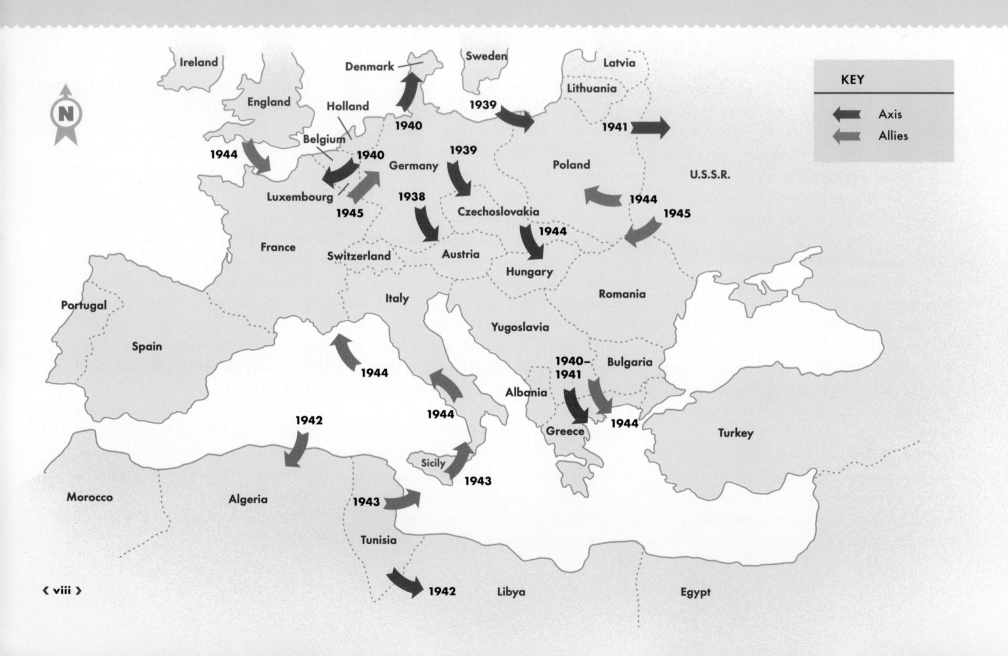

MAP OF THE PACIFIC

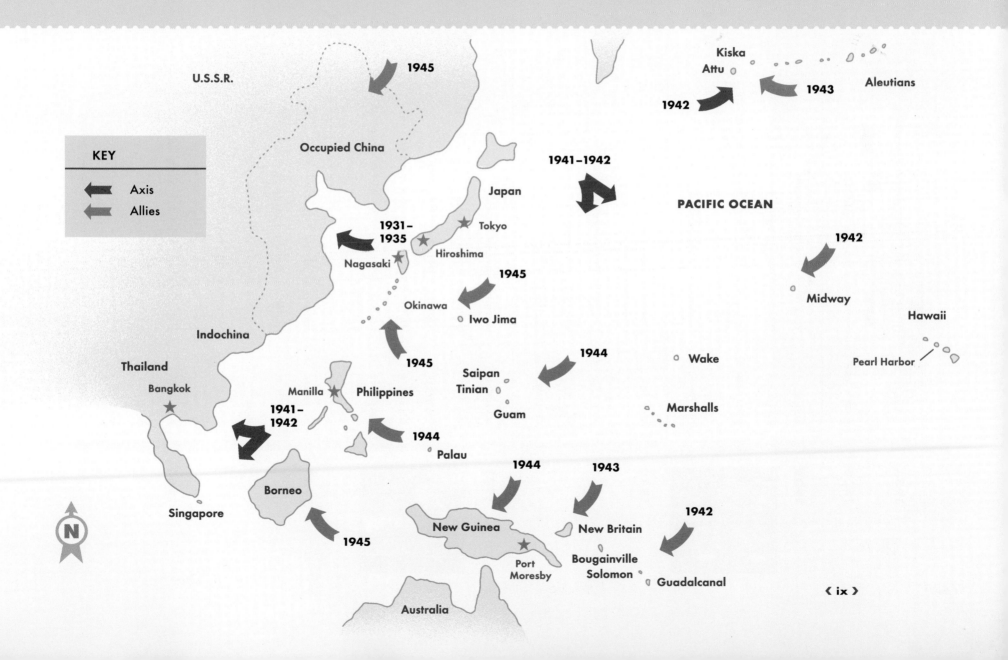

KEY
- Axis
- Allies

U.S.S.R.

Occupied China

Japan

Tokyo

Hiroshima

Nagasaki

Indochina

Thailand

Bangkok

Manilla

Philippines

Singapore

Borneo

Okinawa

Iwo Jima

Saipan
Tinian

Guam

Palau

New Guinea

Port Moresby

New Britain

Bougainville
Solomon

Guadalcanal

Australia

Kiska
Attu

Aleutians

PACIFIC OCEAN

Midway

Hawaii

Pearl Harbor

Wake

Marshalls

N

1945
1942
1943
1941–1942
1931–1935
1945
1945
1945
1944
1944
1944
1943
1942
1942
1941–1942

TIME LINE

1933
- JANUARY 30 — Hitler becomes chancellor of Germany

1938
- MARCH 13 — Germans take over Austria

1939
- AUGUST 23 — Russian pact with Germans
- SEPTEMBER 1 — Germans invade Poland
- SEPTEMBER 3 — Great Britain and France declare war on Germany
- NOVEMBER 30 — Russians invade Finland

1940
- MAY 10 — Germans invade Holland, Belgium, Luxemburg
- MAY 26–JUNE 4 — Evacuation at Dunkirk
- MAY 28 — Belgium surrenders to Germany
- SEPTEMBER 27 — Japan joins Axis

1941
- MARCH 13 — Germans invade Egypt
- JUNE 22 — Germans invade Russia
- DECEMBER 7 — Japanese bomb Pearl Harbor
- DECEMBER 8 — United States declares war on Japan
- DECEMBER 11 — United States declares war on Germany and Italy

1942
- DECEMBER 13 — Japanese invade Guam
- MARCH 20 — Rangoon, Burma, falls to Japanese
- JUNE 7 — Japanese defeated at Midway
- JUNE 12 — Japanese land on Aleutian Islands

1943
- FEBRUARY 2 — Germans surrender at Stalingrad
- JULY 10 — Allies land on Sicily
- JULY 25 — Mussolini quits
- SEPTEMBER 3 — Italy surrenders to Allies (but fighting continues)

1944

JUNE 4	Rome falls to Allies
JUNE 6	D-Day
JUNE 15	Americans invade Saipan
JULY 20	Americans invade Guam
AUGUST 25	Paris liberated
SEPTEMBER 10	Americans invade Germany
OCTOBER 17	MacArthur returns to the Philippines
DECEMBER 16	German counteroffensive in Ardennes begins

1945

FEBRUARY 4	Manila, Philippines, liberated
FEBRUARY 19	Americans invade Iwo Jima
MARCH 7	Allies cross Rhine River
APRIL 1	Americans land at Okinawa
APRIL 12	Roosevelt dies
APRIL 13	Vienna falls to Russians
APRIL 22	Russians invade Berlin
APRIL 28	Mussolini executed
APRIL 30	Hitler commits suicide
MAY 7	Germany surrenders
MAY 8	V-E (Europe) Day
JUNE 22	Battle for Okinawa ends
JULY 1	Australians land at Balikpapan, Borneo in last amphibious invasion of war
JULY 7	Philippines completely liberated
AUGUST 6	Atomic bomb dropped on Hiroshima, Japan
AUGUST 8	Russia declares war on Japan, crosses into Manchuria
AUGUST 9	Atomic bomb dropped on Nagasaki
AUGUST 15	Japan surrenders
SEPTEMBER 2	V-J (Japan) Day; Japanese surrender to Allies aboard USS Missouri

A WORLD AT WAR

>> Throughout the 1920s, everyone in the world was aware of the terrible price of the First World War. Though it ended in 1918, many people were fearful that another war could easily start over a relatively minor disagreement. Germany, the main aggressor of World War I, was punished severely by the Allies—the United States, France, and England—who won the war. As part of the Treaty of Versailles of June 28, 1919,

★ ★ ★ ★ ★ ★ ★ ★ ★ ★

Germany had to pay large fines and was not allowed to manufacture any weapons. Inflation made German money worthless after the war. People went hungry. Disease ravaged the population. The political situation in Germany was chaotic. New political parties were formed to oppose the ruling government. One of these was called the Nazi Party.

The Nazis were a strongly patriotic, anti-Communist party whose name was short for the National Socialist German Worker's Party. Founded in 1920, the Nazi Party was eventually led by a failed Austrian artist named Adolf Hitler. The Nazis believed Germany had to be rebuilt regardless of what the Treaty of Versailles said. The French, a major enemy of the Germans in World War I, were very concerned about the neighbors who had invaded their country so many times over the years.

While Germany suffered greatly in the years after World War I, many people in the United States were still bitter about being dragged into the war at the cost of $32 billion and at the loss of 50,000 lives. Though in 1920 the Americans had helped create the League of Nations, an early form of the United Nations, President Woodrow Wilson could not get support in Congress and the United States did not join the League. Most Americans were content to have their country stay out of world politics. This policy was called "isolationism."

Still, when France called on America to sign a pact banning wars, the United States was interested. Why not invite other countries to participate? After some discussion, the question was settled. In August 1928 the United States and France were joined by 13 other countries in signing the Kellogg-Briand Pact, named after the Secretary of State of the United States, Frank B. Kellogg, and the foreign minister of France, Aristide Briand.

The idea of the pact was to outlaw war: " . . . [the diplomats signing the pact] solemnly declare in the names of their respective peoples that they condemn . . . war for the solution of international controversies, and renounce it . . . [and] agree that the settlement or solution of all disputes or conflicts of whatever nature or of whatever origin they may be, which may arise among them, shall never be sought except by pacific [peaceful] means." Eventually, about 60 countries signed the pact, including Italy, Japan, Germany, and the Soviet Union. Nobody in the United States foresaw that within a few years, several of the signing countries would violate the pact.

The Great Depression

American hopes for world peace were soon overshadowed by a new concern. On Tuesday, October 29, 1929, the value of the New York stock market fell and, in a panic, people around the country rushed to their banks to withdraw all their money. The banks, having also suffered badly from the crash, could not pay everyone who wanted their money. So began the Great Depression in America.

Once prosperous, Americans now struggled to make ends meet. Farmers could not make enough money because crop prices tumbled. Jobs were scarce, and many families did not have enough money to pay for their basic needs. By the end of 1932, nearly 100,000 businesses had collapsed. The presidential election of 1932 pitted Republican President Herbert Hoover against former New York governor Franklin Delano Roosevelt, a Democrat. Americans decided that they were ready for a change and voted in Roosevelt as the 32nd President.

Over the next several years, President Roosevelt did much to help his country get back on its feet. In 1936 he won reelection by a landslide. Roosevelt started many federal programs aimed at assisting the needy and putting "a chicken in every pot," as he promised. Because

many people had lost almost all their money, Roosevelt created the Federal Deposit Insurance Corporation (FDIC), a plan that insured bank deposits against future bank closings. Overall, in the 1930s Americans were focused on fixing their own problems. Through the early and mid-1930s, hoping to avoid major involvement in world politics, Roosevelt participated warily in world affairs.

Trouble Abroad

Meanwhile, trouble was brewing in Europe. For years Hitler had tried to gain power in Germany, and, in November 1923, he staged an attempt to overthrow the government by holding hostage the leaders of a rival political party who had been meeting at a beer hall. For this attempt he was thrown into prison for a short time. While in prison he wrote *Mein Kampf*, a political philosophy that laid out many of his ideas about Germany's superiority. Through the late 1920s, the Nazi Party's influence slowly grew, but not enough to attract the attention of the world. By 1928 the Nazis had only a few seats in the Reichstag, or German parliament.

Things changed quickly, though. In 1930, after inflation and high unemployment hit Germany, elections gave the Communists 13 percent

➤ **Adolf Hitler (right) with Dr. Otto Dietrich, head of the Nazi Press Agency and publicity agent for Hitler.**

their allegiance to Hitler, and the Nazis took complete control of the government. Hitler continued to have Communist and Socialist leaders arrested, and finally he was able to declare that the Nazi Party was to be the only legal party in Germany. Teams of his specially trained black-shirted "protection team," the *Schutz Staffel* (SS), roamed the streets. Hitler was now in a position to begin the rearmament of Germany.

As the world eyed Germany cautiously, there were already signs that the new Nazi government would spell big trouble for world peace. In 1936, in defiance of the Versailles Treaty, Hitler militarized the Rhineland, the area of Germany along the west banks of the Rhine River. Hitler quickly gained complete support of the people in Germany. By 1936 almost 99 percent of the people said they had confidence in him—few dared oppose him. To restore pride in Germany and also to create loyalty to the Nazi Party, Hitler organized youth groups. German boys and girls, some as young as six years old, were encouraged to join these groups. Many of these youths joined the army when they grew up and fought during the war in France, Poland, and Russia. Most of them did not have a choice. In March 1935, service in the German Army became mandatory for all German men of military age. In June 1935, it became a law that German men who turned 20 had to join the *Arbeitsdienst* (work service) to help build roads or construct buildings for six months

of the vote and the Nazis 18 percent. In the 1932 elections, President Hindenburg received 53 percent of the vote and Hitler, 37 percent. Giving in to pressure, Hindenburg appointed Hitler as chancellor on January 30, 1933. The German people, of whom millions were unemployed, were eager for a leader who could take them into prosperity. Meanwhile, on February 27, 1933, the Reichstag building broke out in flames. The German Communists were blamed for the fire, and several thousand were arrested.

By July 1933 Hitler's power was much greater than Hindenburg's. After the elderly Hindenburg died in August 1934, the military swore to prepare for service in the army. By the end of the year almost 600,000 young German men had been called into army service. Each year hundreds of thousands more German men were drafted. Factories turned out new planes, warships, and weapons at an alarming rate.

The building of an air force and the enforcement of an army draft were both violations of the Treaty of Versailles. In April 1935, a German official said, "The necessity of a new European peace conference to replace the Versailles Treaty has long been evident . . . [but if the new conference] is predicated upon . . . an agenda inconsistent with Germany's position and policies, much of its value and effort would pale immediately."

Though the American government was not very interested in becoming involved in world politics, the American people were well aware of the situation in Europe. The *New York Evening Journal* of April 11, 1935, had several stories about the crisis. Across the front page in bold headlines was written, "France Will Meet With Hitler." Inside were several articles on possible upcoming peace talks. There was also a story about a proposed student antiwar strike organized by the National Student Strike Committee, which hoped to convince 50,000 students to strike as a way to "protest the world armament race."

In 1935 Mussolini had sent troops into a part of Africa known then as Abyssinia, now Ethiopia.

The League of Nations told Italy it was in violation of the rules, but Italy requested that it be allowed to resolve the crisis with the Ethiopian government alone and not go through the League of Nations, to which Ethiopia had sent a complaint.

As Germany rearmed and grew stronger, Hitler became greedy for more territory. Hitler, like Benito Mussolini in Italy, was a Fascist. The Fascists believed in absolute power for a

➤ **Nazi swearing-in ceremony in the city of Braunschweig, Germany, 1936. Note the picture of Hitler in front of the giant swastika.**

dictator and in expansion of their countries and exploitation of other countries, even at the expense of lives. In 1937 Hitler and Mussolini agreed to form the Rome–Berlin Axis, a partnership that laid the foundation for the Fascist takeover of Europe. Both countries had an interest in the Spanish Civil War, begun in 1936. This war pitted the government of Spain against rebels led by the Fascist General Francisco Franco. Both Germany and Italy provided Franco's forces with aid.

At this point President Roosevelt was still trying to keep America out of the mess in Europe, but he saw that it would be wise to prepare for war anyway. He asked Congress for a billion-dollar program to build up the United States fleet of warships. Hitler invaded Austria in March 1938, claiming it was a natural thing for these two countries to be joined because the people, the language, and the heritage were the same. An Austrian by birth, Hitler had long dreamed of the day when the two countries could be united. With his appetite for more land still not satisfied, Hitler next announced that he wanted to take over a part of neighboring Czechoslovakia called the Sudetenland. The excuse was that this part of Czechoslovakia was heavily populated by German-speaking people.

The Prime Minister of Britain, Neville Chamberlain, went to Munich, Germany, to try to talk some sense into Hitler. Instead, Chamberlain wound up agreeing to let Hitler take over the Sudetenland, as long as it was the last territory he would take. Chamberlain thought that the appeasement of Hitler would create good feeling between Germany and the rest of Europe, but he was wrong. Hitler, still hungry for more territory, took over the rest of Czechoslovakia in March 1939. President Roosevelt, growing more alarmed, sent a personal message of concern to Hitler in April 1939, but received no reply.

Dark Clouds
Eva A., born 1919

On March 10, 1938, Eva gave birth to a baby daughter in Budapest, the capital of Hungary. She was in the Fasor sanitorium, a small hospital, recuperating for the next week. As pleasant and quiet as it was inside, she felt the world was turning very black outside. Since she had just given birth, nobody wanted to upset her by telling her that Germany had invaded Austria on March 12, and it did not look good for the rest of Europe. Though they tried to be cheerful and hide their concern, she remembers seeing the worry in the faces of her husband, brother-in-law, and mother-in-law when they came to visit her and the baby. "We hoped that we would be excluded from Hitler's stupidity, but we somehow knew that sooner or later it would come to us," she said.

After the war started, her husband insisted on listening to Hitler's speeches on the radio, even though Eva did not want to hear them. He thought it was important to keep informed about the situation in Europe. He and his friends always discussed Germany and Europe when they met at parties or gatherings. Eva hated hearing Hitler shouting his threats over the radio. She remembers feeling very frightened when he yelled, *"Wir werden Euere Städte aus radieren!"* ("We will erase all your cities!") Even 60 years later, she can still hear his menacing voice in her head.

The German American Bund
Howard S., born 1925

Though many Americans were appalled at the actions of Hitler and his Nazi Party, there were some who supported Germany. In 1937 a group called the German American Bund was formed, with its headquarters in New Jersey. This *Bund* (association) was made up of Americans of German descent who were proud of their heritage and who also supported Hitler.

Howard, who was about 14 years old at the time, remembers that one branch of the Bund had meetings not far from where he grew up in Queens, New York. The group of at least 100 people were dressed in uniforms with swastikas, and they carried Nazi flags. He could hear them swearing their allegiance to Hitler in German and performing their drills behind their fenced-in meeting grounds. Howard recalled that in February 1939 the Bund even had a huge rally at Madison Square Garden that attracted about 20,000 people.

At that time many Americans were not too interested in the situation abroad. "This isn't our war. That's over there, with an ocean between us," he remembers some people's sentiment being before America entered the war. Within a few years, the Bund was outlawed in the United States as anti-German sentiment grew strong.

A World at War

Hitler was still not satisfied. He wanted control over the parts of Poland that had large German populations. Many of the towns and villages in western Poland had both German names and Polish names because they once were part of Prussia, a German territory. But as with Czechoslovakia, Hitler never intended to stop. He wanted to control all of Poland. He knew that Britain and France would declare war on Germany if the Nazis invaded Poland. In order to succeed, Hitler knew he had to strike an agreement with the Soviet Union before Britain and France tried the same thing. If he could get the leader of the Soviet Union, Joseph Stalin, to agree to a nonaggression pact, it would mean the

➤ A Nazi propaganda poster that proclaims "workers are the frontline soldiers of Hitler."

Russians would sit by and not take any action to stop him. On August 23, 1939, Hitler's foreign minister, Joachim von Ribbentrop, signed an agreement with Stalin's foreign minister, Yacheslav Molotov. It was a coup for Hitler and Germany. The Germans were so giddy that there was even a political song played on the radio that went: *"Hast kein Gluck beim Stalin Chamberlain"*—Chamberlain had no luck with Stalin.

The world was in shock. On August 24, 1939, Roosevelt wrote a note to Hitler: "I therefore urge with all earnestness—and I am likewise urging the President of the Republic of Poland that the Governments of Germany and Poland agree by common accord to refrain from any positive act of hostility for a reasonable and stipulated period, and that they agree likewise by common accord to solve the controversies which have arisen between them . . . I appeal to you in the name of the people of the United States, and I believe in the name of peace loving men and women everywhere . . . " Roosevelt also wrote to the president of Poland on the same day, assuring him that he believed that "the rank and file of every nation—large and small—want peace."

The communication had no effect on Hitler, and on September 1, 1939, the German army invaded Poland. Two days later, on September 3, Britain and France declared war on Germany, as promised. On September 5 Roosevelt declared the United States' neutrality. Still, Americans wanted to protect their interests. The countries in North and South America met soon after and on October 3 came up with the Act of Panama. The act called for neutral zones extending from the shoreline of the Americas a few hundred miles into the ocean. All countries of the world were warned against any hostile actions within that neutral zone.

Having made peace with Hitler, Stalin had his own plans for expansion and decided to take action next. He sent the Red Army into Finland for what turned out to be a difficult and bloody struggle. Meanwhile, now that war had begun, Hitler continued his quest to control all of Europe. He planned to strike quickly and con-

➤ **German soldiers in field training, circa 1939. Notice the machine gun they are about to fire.**

quer most of Western Europe in a few weeks. The main target was Germany's old adversary, France.

Growing Up in Nazi Germany

Helga S., born 1929

"One morning early in September 1939, my mother came upstairs to wake up my brother and me, but there would be no school. German troops had invaded Poland and there was to be a school holiday. We jumped up and down on our beds, planning on what to do on this unexpected day of freedom! My brother was seven, and I was nine years old. Mostly we played on our street with the neighborhood kids: dodge ball or marbles or rode our bicycles. Our parents reacted quite differently and there was a lot of talk about the war of 1914 to 1918, when they were our age. Not much changed right away and people talked about it being all over by Christmas.

"But then fathers, uncles, and neighbors were drafted. Some went to fight the war at the front, others to build roads and police the conquered lands. Gradually there was less to buy in the stores, then there was rationing. You got coupons for one pair of shoes a year and also for foodstuff. Private cars had to be given up. But we had to go back to school and there were always geography lessons, maps with little flags on the areas in the news. And, of course, the bullies in school and the neighborhood who said, 'We beat them! Let's play war!' Both my brother and I

were too young and anyhow not interested in joining the Hitler youth group."

 Just because Hitler had big plans, it did not mean that German and Austrian soldiers were happy to be taken away from their homes and families and made to fight in a war of aggression.

✠

Today is mother's birthday and it is the first time since the years of [the First] World War that I cannot be with her [the letter writer must have served in World War I, also]. And because this absence was caused by others, I feel especially bad about it. I can be with her only in my thoughts, can only send her my kisses and ask her forgiveness that I am not with her. As soon as I am set free I will make up for it a thousand times. That I promise and that promise I will keep. This morning I got from the army post office the package with the newspapers you sent ... As already reported, I have doubts to be able to come for Christmas. That would mean Christmas at the front! However, I certainly hope that it won't be long before I come home, hope, hope, hope! ... It's a pity but I cannot buy

★ Airplane Design

By World War II airplane technology had come a long way since its infancy 40 years earlier. The new planes were much sleeker and faster than the first planes. Scientists worked hard to streamline the planes and reduce drag. To streamline something is to design it so that air flows easily around it, instead of creating resistance. Try pushing the palm of your hand through a tub of water or in a swimming pool. Can you feel the resistance? Observe the little eddies of water created behind your hand as you push it through the water. This is called *drag*. These eddies, or currents of water, make it more difficult to propel your hand. If you turn your hand so that it slices it through the water, you can feel how much easier it is to move. An airplane will travel faster and more easily if it is streamlined; that is, designed with a minimum number of surfaces that can cause resistance

and drag. A smooth, slender, and angular surface passes through the air more easily.

When designing airplanes, engineers also had to make sure that the wings were curved on the top sides. Air travels around the wings at different speeds. It travels a little faster above the wings and a little slower below, making the air pressure below

the wings a little higher than the pressure above the wings. This helps lift the airplane. When the wings are slightly tilted, the air hitting the underside of the wings also makes an impact and the force of the impact on the underside of the wings pushes upward. The two forces, lift and impact, combine to help lift the airplane into the air.

[b]

[c]

[a]

➤ Allied airplanes of World War II included: [a] Curtiss *Cleveland*: a United States Navy biplane that was sent to England when the war started; [b] Vultee *Vengeance*: A British dive bomber and attack bomber; [c] Boeing *Flying Fortress*: A workhorse bomber could carry 10 tons of bombs; [d] Lockheed *Hudson*: Ordered by the British from the United States, and then included in Lend Lease, it played a role in the evacuation at Dunkirk in 1940; [e] Grumman *Avenger*: A superb torpedo plane, used for the dangerous mission of attacking enemy ships; saw action at the battle of Midway in 1942; [f] Martin *Marauder*: A medium bomber; at war's end had the lowest loss rate of any USAAF bomber.

[d]

[e]

[f]

anything here and I also do not know how it will be with the traffic for the holidays. It would be a sad Christmas. Wish it would be over! ... In any case, there is progress. Now it is to be hoped that what they are writing in the newspapers will be implemented and we "old timers" will be sent home soon!

Letter from a soldier to his father Otto in Vienna

December 9, 1939

The U-Boat War

The submarine had been perfected in the early 20th century and played a role in the First World War. The World War II submarine was a hollow steel shell with minimally comfortable living quarters for a crew. Submarines laid mines underwater and also shot torpedoes, their main purpose. Through a metal tube-like device called a periscope, barely noticeable on the surface of the water, the submarine crew could spot ships from a distance, then quickly descend and get close enough to the hull of the ship to fire a torpedo. These self-propelled capsules were built with engines and propellers and sped through the water toward their targets. They were capped with high explosives that would blow up when they made contact with another ship. Subs could cruise at fast speeds on the surface of the ocean, but once submerged, they could only travel about as fast as you can run. Because it was dangerous for a submarine to stay on the surface, for fear of being spotted by the enemy, submarine crews spent most of their time cooped up in a small space with no fresh air or light of day. World War II submarines were more than 200 feet (60 m) long, had a crew of about 40, and could dive up to 400 feet (120 m) below the water's surface.

By the time Germany invaded Poland on September 1, 1939, a fleet of German submarines was already in the water, cruising near the coast of Great Britain. The German submarines were known as U-boats, *Unterseeboote* or "under-sea boats," and each one was known by its own number; for example, U-1 through U-6 were training submarines.

As soon as Britain declared war on Germany on September 3, 1939, word was given to the German submarine commanders to attack enemy ships. In what may have been a mistake, a passenger ship called the *Athenia* was torpedoed and destroyed by the German U-30, with a loss of 118 lives. The ship carried 1,418 Jewish refugees, as well as Americans and British passengers. By

September 30, more than 40 ships had been sunk by U-boats. This marked the beginning of a six-year-long U-boat war that pitted British and American naval escorts, especially destroyers, against German U-boats.

Unlike the land war, submarine warfare did not always seek to kill people. In fact, after firing the initial torpedoes that disabled Allied freighters, U-boat captains sometimes tried to make sure the ships' crews were in lifeboats before firing the fatal torpedo that sank the ship. Submarine kills were measured by the size of the ship that was sunk. Each ship weighed many tons and was expensive to build. Steel was especially precious during wartime, as was the cargo of the freighters—oil, food, or other merchandise. The more large ships sunk, the bigger the effect on the enemy's economy and morale. The first German U-boat captain to reach the 100,000-ton-mark received an Iron Cross award from Hitler. Over the course of the war, hundreds of Allied ships weighing a total of more than 21,000,000 tons were sunk by U-boats.

The safest way for ships to travel was in convoys of several ships. Traveling alone was dangerous and accounted for most of the ships lost. Submarines stayed away from convoys because they were more likely to have armed escorts that could find and destroy U-boats. After a few American ships were sunk or damaged in 1941, Congress authorized merchant ships to carry arms and authorized the navy to fire on U-boats, though the United States was still neutral at that time.

Over the course of the war, more than 40,000 men served on U-boats. Just as with airplanes, there were some submarine captains who were "aces" and made many kills, while others went through the war without sinking any ships. Life was not easy for U-boat crews. Special ships called destroyers cruised the surface waters of the Atlantic. These destroyers were equipped with the technology to locate submarines and drop explosive charges on them, thus destroying them. Once located from the surface, a submarine's slow speed underwater made escape difficult. German U-boats, while successful in sinking many ships during the war, had a high casualty rate. More than 30,000 of the people who served on German U-boats were either killed or captured.

Blitzkrieg!

In September 1939, most of the might of the German army was concentrated in the east for the invasion of Poland. In just days most of the Polish air force was reduced to ruined heaps of molten metal. Many planes never even had a chance to take off. Powerful German tanks rolled across the Polish countryside by the hundreds. The complete defeat of Poland took less than a month. German army divisions pushed into Poland from the west and squeezed around the last concentrations of Polish resistance in a "pincers" movement. Meanwhile, the Russians helped the Germans by invading from the east. On September 29, a treaty to split Poland between the Soviet Union and Germany was signed. Murdering millions of innocent civilians, the Nazis showed no mercy during the Polish campaign and the nearly six-year occupation that followed.

After Poland was secured by the German army, Hitler felt confident that he could transfer many of those troops back west and focus on building up an invasion army to take over Western Europe. A winter of relative quiet and uneasiness on the part of the Allies was followed by a disastrous spring. On April 9, 1940, Germany invaded Denmark and Norway. There was panic in the governments of Britain and France. By May 1940, Hitler had 126 army divisions waiting near the border with Holland, Belgium, and France. The French and Belgians, along with British support, called the British Expeditionary Force or BEF, were also building up troops along the border with Germany. In fact, they had nearly the same number of divisions as the Germans did, ready in case of attack. But the Germans had the advantage of surprise—nobody knew when or where the first attack would take

➤ **Photos of the invasion of France in 1940, left to right: A German division is ready to invade France, June 1940. German soldiers climbing the ruins of destroyed benzine (fuel) storage tanks in France. Devastation in northeastern France, June 1940. Makeshift graves of German soldiers killed in action, 1940.**

place. They made their first move on the night of May 9 and 10, charging across the border and into Holland, Belgium, and Luxembourg. Flames lit up the sky from the bombing by German planes. The combination of massive numbers of heavily armored tanks and the menace from the German bombers proved too much for the Allies.

The British were eager to help fight the Nazis. At the same time, they were reluctant to send too many troops and planes to France, because Britain would be left with inadequate defense. At the order of King Leopold of Belgium, the Belgian army surrendered on May 28, surprising the French and British and making retreat for

them more difficult. Meanwhile, the French army was being beaten by the Germans. Once the German army had poked a hole in the Allied lines, they were able to get through into France. Chances of the Allies winning the battle for France were growing slimmer day by day.

Winston Churchill, newly appointed as prime minister, recognized that if British troops remained in France, they risked being captured or killed. Then, who would be left to defend Britain against German attack? It was decided that the BEF troops would try to make their way to the French coast for evacuation back to Britain.

It was a risky plan, because the Germans had already pierced their way into France and were

beginning to surround the Allied forces. Nonetheless, the dangerous march to the sea began. On May 26 the evacuations started. Though at first there were not very many ships taking part in the rescue operation, every kind of boat imaginable was called into service during the next few days. Fishing boats, tugboats, and lifeboats were all used to ferry troops across the choppy English Channel under constant risk of German bombardment by air. Not only was the trip across the Channel difficult, keeping German troops away from Dunkirk was also a struggle. About 50,000 French troops fought gallantly to fend off the Germans, but finally were forced to surrender on May 31.

The evacuation was a success, but there were many losses. While men were saved, equipment was not. More than 100,000 vehicles, many thousands of guns, and thousands of tons of ammunition were left behind. More than one-quarter of the 861 boats used in the rescue operation were sunk by the Germans. Still, as of June 4, 1940, the end of the operation, more than 338,000 troops, including French troops, were saved from German capture and delivered safely to England, leaving only 68,000 dead, injured, or captured. Churchill made a speech to Parliament in which he praised the triumph of Dunkirk, but also warned the British people not to be too relieved, saying that "Wars are not won by evacuations." There was still a long fight ahead.

After Dunkirk, the Germans refocused on continuing their push into France. The remaining French and British forces regrouped along the line of advancement and were soon assisted by more troops sent in from Britain and Canada. Still, the Germans advanced rapidly, driving toward Paris. Between June 5 and June 11, they advanced as much as 50 miles (80 km) in some places, within striking distance of Paris. The overpowered and exhausted French troops were unable to keep the Nazis back. The German army entered Paris on June 14, 1940. The leader of France soon resigned, not wishing to remain in charge of a France occupied by the enemy. A new leader of France was appointed, Marshall Philip Petain, the 84-year-old World War I hero. Petain immediately asked for an armistice with Germany.

The Blitz and the Battle of Britain

The British had every reason to fear another war. During the First World War, German bombs killed more than 1,000 British people, and that was when airplane technology was still in its infancy. As time passed, and Germany headed toward rearmament, the British government began to grow concerned. Soon it was clear that Germany's rebuilt air force, known as the *Luftwaffe*, was equal in strength to the British Royal Air Force (RAF). An "air parade," held in Berlin on Hitler's birthday in 1935, caused concern in England and led to increased production of fighter and bomber planes. Even by the time Hitler took power in 1933, plans were already in the works for the protection of the British population from an attack. It was calculated that more than 500,000 people might be killed if Hitler's air force attacked the British Isles.

Battle of Britain
Anita W., born 1923

Anita was 17 years old and living on her own in London when the heavy air raids began. She remembers the bombing of London and how brave the British people were. "The bombs were falling. You get up in the morning and have a cup of tea. They were very stubborn; it's their nature to carry on. There was no excitement. Everybody went along and did the best they could." On one occasion, Anita had a very close call: "I was supposed to take a certain bus, and I was late, and I had to take another bus to go to work, and that bus [the one she missed] was hit by a bomb, so it was just fate. I was near the airport at Norwich and we watched the dogfights between the [British] Spitfires and the Germans."

In order to prevent this mass destruction, many precautions were taken. Since poison gas was one of the biggest concerns, the government issued instructions to the British people and began to manufacture 44,000,000 gas masks. Bomb shelters were built and fighter planes, ground-based antiaircraft guns, and large search-lights, with a range of 5 miles (8 km) were built at a rapid pace. Along hundreds of miles of the southern and southeastern coast of England, radar stations were built to give advance warning of incoming German planes. The radar stations sent radio waves into the air that were bounced back when they hit something, so incoming aircraft could be detected by a spike in the display of jagged lines on the radar screens. This allowed the RAF to send fighter planes into the sky to defend their country.

In another measure to protect themselves, numerous giant "barrage" balloons were floated in a circle around the perimeter of London. Each balloon was tied to the ground and to the other balloons by steel cables that would form a "death trap" for fighter planes attempting to fly past them.

The boldest part of the British defense plan was the evacuation of millions of citizens from crowded cities and coastal towns, the most obvious targets, to suburbs and country towns. Beginning in December 1939, more than 3,000,000 people were successfully evacuated by

➤ Above: A spotlight searches the British skies for enemy aircraft. Right: Barrage balloons over London.

train and bus. This measure saved countless thousands of lives. More than 1,000,000 of all the evacuees were children. Many of these children were sent far away to small villages. They waited in groups for the local villagers to claim them one by one. At the same time, because they were thought to be a security threat, about 27,000 Germans and Italians living in Britain were placed in camps by July 1940.

During the summer of 1940, the Germans were considering landing their forces in England, a plan code-named Operation Sea Lion. This never happened because the Germans lost a fierce Battle of Britain, July 10 to October 31, in the skies over England. Intense bombing by the *Luftwaffe* continued for several months before the British forces were finally triumphant. The Germans had not counted on British victory, which came at the steep cost of one in every three

Extinguish an Incendiary

The British people feared air attack by Germany in the event of a war, but ordinary bombs were not their only fear. Incendiary bombs were small and lightweight, only 2 pounds (0.9 kg), but deadly. Instead of exploding, their goal was to start fires and create lots of smoke. They could crash into attics and within minutes, set an entire house on fire. Still, unlike exploding bombs, incendiaries at least gave people a chance to minimize the destruction these bombs caused. Instructions were given to the British people on how to extinguish and dispose of these bombs before they caused too much damage. This activity recreates the actual steps you were supposed to take in case an incendiary landed in your house. The equipment has been modified from the original scoop and hoe kit to household items you can easily find.

MATERIALS
* Connected garden hose
* Plastic bucket filled about halfway with sand or dirt
* Long-handled shovel
* Long-handled broom
* Potato

Note: This activity *does not* involve the use of fire.

➤ British woman demonstrates the proper way to extinguish an incendiary bomb.

Find a place outdoors where you can be near the garden hose. Place the bucket of sand on its side so the sand is easily accessible. Set the potato, which takes the place of the "incendiary bomb," about 10 feet (3 m) away. Kneel down low to the ground to avoid the "smoke" that would come from a real bomb. Turn on the hose and spray the potato for 10 seconds. This would put out the "fire." In reality, the water would be sprayed from something called a "stirrup hand pump" placed into a bucket of water. Now, scoop some sand out of the bucket with the shovel and pour it onto the "bomb." This would cool the bomb down and allow it to be handled more safely. Next, use the broom to sweep the bomb into the shovel. Then lift the shovel over to the bucket and deposit the bomb into the bucket. The bomb can then be carried away from the house.

British pilots killed. In fact, if the Germans had continued their bombing of British air bases for much longer, England would most likely have lost the Battle of Britain, setting up the possibility of a land invasion.

London was one of the biggest German targets because of its large population and its location close to the English Channel, making German getaways easier. Industrial cities were also targets. After the Battle of Britain, daytime bombing ceased, but there was still occasional nighttime bombing. By the time the Germans surrendered in 1945, more than 60,000 British civilians had been killed by air raids.

Lend Lease

The United States was finding it more and more difficult to stay neutral as the war progressed. President Roosevelt regularly received notes from the new British Prime Minister, Winston Churchill. In these letters, Churchill explained how dismal things looked and asked the United States for help. The United States was able to send Britain 100 old bombers when the war started, a drop in the bucket, but still a sign of Roosevelt's willingness to help. As France was being attacked in May 1940, Churchill wrote that "if American assistance is to play any part, it must be available soon." In early September 1940, Roosevelt was finally able to offer more assistance. In exchange for a 99-year lease on eight British-owned naval and air bases, the United States sent Britain 50 old destroyers.

Fascism in Italy

Mario S., born 1907

Mario was a scientist and engineer who worked with Enrico Fermi (1901–1954), the world-famous physicist who built the world's first nuclear reactor. Mario got an idea of what Mussolini was up to when he was in the Italian army as a young man. His colonel ordered him to shoot down a plane dropping anti-Fascist leaflets over Rome. Mario was opposed to the order for two reasons—first, because he had anti-Fascist feelings himself and second, he realized that the old World War I shells that they were using might explode and kill innocent people before reaching their target. He told the four sergeants under his command, "Whether the plane appears, whether we get orders from the general command, you do not shoot until I say shoot." Luckily, the "enemy" plane never appeared in the skies that night and Mario did not have to make the judgment call that could have landed him in serious trouble.

When Mario went to England to study engineering, he was exposed to the truth about Mussolini and what the outside world thought of fascism. After that

trip, Mario subscribed to the *London Times* so he could keep track of outside opinions of Mussolini's actions.

In the late 1930s Mario won a grant to go to the United States to study the development of television. He visited his colleague Enrico Fermi to ask for a recommendation. Fermi told him, "I'm not writing any letters!" As it turned out, Fermi was too busy to write a letter for Mario. He was just about to travel to Sweden with his wife and children to pick up the Nobel Prize in physics and then go on to America, never to return to Italy. Another physicist looked into

➤ The constant rain of German bombs in 1940 did not crush the spirit of the British people, who tried to carry on with their lives as best they could.

➤ **Unloading Thompson submachine guns that arrived in England from the United States as part of Lend-Lease.**

the room and asked what was going on. Fermi told him that both he and Mario were leaving. The third man said, "What am I, an idiot? I'm leaving too!" Many of Italy and Germany's top scientists fled during the 1930s because of their anti-Fascist feelings.

Once in the United States, Mario got a job teaching at a prestigious university. On the day in December 1941 when Italy declared war on the United States, a woman working with him offered to lend him $500 in case his bank accounts were suspended. The head of the department came in and told him, "As far as we are concerned, you're Dr. S. and we don't care where you are from." Mario was told he could be paid in cash instead of by check by the university if the government seized his bank accounts. In the end, the American government did not do anything against Italian Americans. Mario soon began to write anti-Fascist pamphlets, which were distributed to Italian partisans. He campaigned for Roosevelt in Spanish Harlem, New York. He was also a member of the anti-Mussolini Italian underground group *Giustizia e Liberta* (Justice and Liberty), founded in 1929 in Paris and active in several countries around the world.

Roosevelt's authority as president did not go as far as he would have liked. He needed approval from Congress to really help the British. Roosevelt made his case with the American people in radio speeches such as the one on December 30, 1940, when he warned that if Britain fell, it would mean America "would be living at the point of a gun." Under growing pressure the opposition to foreign aid finally caved in, and in March 1941 the American government approved assistance to any country that needed help. This bill was called the Lend-Lease Act. The Act stated: "The President may . . . whenever he deems it in the interest of national defense . . . authorize the Secretary of War . . . to manufacture . . . any defense article for the government of any country whose defense the President deems vital to the defense of the United States."

This act allowed Roosevelt to provide Churchill, and other Allies, with the help he so desperately needed to get an edge on the Germans. Within the first nine months, more than $2 billion in defense shipments were sent, mostly to Britain.

Meanwhile, in September 1940, Mussolini's army had invaded Egypt. The British sent troops to Africa to battle the Italians, and in March 1941 they recaptured the territory, next to Ethiopia, called Italian Somaliland. In April the British secured Ethiopia. Because Italy was having trouble in Africa, Hitler decided to send support. His choice to lead the troops in Africa was a talented general named Erwin Rommel, known as "The Desert Fox." Rommel would soon become one of the most famous figures of the war.

Operation Barbarossa

Although in 1939 Germany and Russia had agreed not to attack each other, things changed rapidly. Uneasiness and territorial misunderstandings caused the Soviet leaders to begin to question Hitler's intentions. But the Soviets were slow to act. There were distractions, such as the Soviet occupation of Latvia and Estonia in June 1940, and also great purges of any military leaders by whom Stalin felt threatened. Slowly, the Soviet Union realized it needed to prepare for its defense, but by then it was too late. By December 1940 Hitler was certain he was going to invade Russia, but he did not know when the invasion would occur. While Soviet leaders were debating the situation, German reconnaissance planes were spying on Soviet installations.

In the spring of 1941 a date was set. Finally, "Operation Barbarossa" was put into action. In the early morning hours of June 22, 1941, Germany invaded the Soviet Union without warning. The invasion army was 3,000,000 men strong and was backed up by more than 3,000 tanks and the Luftwaffe. The Russians were unprepared. Though the Soviet Union had a large army, the swift attack gave the Germans an advantage. The German army also had the advantage of experience—most of the soldiers taking part in the Russian campaign had already fought in either Poland or France or both. Easy previous victories helped make the Germans confident in their fighting abilities. The German Stuka airplanes used their 37 mm cannons to fire at Russian tanks that were often sitting ducks. One Stuka pilot alone destroyed more than 500 Russian tanks during the invasion. Whole villages and towns were burned to the ground and virtually erased from the map. Jews were especially singled out for destruction (see Chapter 6).

Churchill, upon learning of the German invasion, pledged his support to the Soviet Union, saying that anyone who was fighting Hitler was on the Allies' side. President Roosevelt extended the Lend-Lease offer to Russia, and the United States began to supply Stalin's army. Even with outside help, the first year following the invasion was difficult for the Russian soldiers. The German army pushed farther and farther inland and began to close in tightly, forming a noose around the Russian army.

In September 1941 the Germans approached the huge city of Moscow. Russian civilians chipped in to help dig trenches surrounding the capital city, and when winter set in, the German troops were ill-prepared for the freezing weather. The Russians struck at the Germans and pushed them back. Moscow was safe for the moment.

Russia Invaded

Asya D., born 1924

"June 22, 1941, was the grand opening of Minsk Lake. The digging and construction had been going on for about four years. At 4 A.M. on the 22nd, the Germans invaded Russia. It took two days for them to get to Minsk [about 175 miles (280 km) from the Polish border]. All the men who had worked at Minsk Lake were recruited into the army directly at the opening party of the new lake. They did not even have a chance to go home and say good-bye. I come from a large family—eight brothers, four sisters, father and mother. I never saw my brothers again. In two days Minsk was occupied. The Russian army could not protect the city of Minsk because they couldn't mobilize properly. All the men who were recruited were put on trucks and driven inland, but on the way they were bombed heavily and a lot of people were lost."

Pearl Harbor

While the world's attention was on the Great Depression and on the activities of Adolf Hitler in Germany, Japan was becoming a military power. In 1931, two years before Hitler's rise to power, the Japanese army invaded the Chinese province of Manchuria. Protest by the Chinese resulted in the city of Shanghai being bombed by the Japanese. Over the next several years, the Japanese pushed farther into China. By March 1933 they had reached the Great Wall of China. By the end of 1938 Japan had control over the most strategic areas of China along the coast. In September 1940 Japan signed an alliance with Germany and Italy and became part of the Axis. Just like Germany and Italy, Japan wanted to continue to expand its power. The United States learned that the Japanese were not planning to stop at China but wanted to keep going until they had control over all of southeast Asia. The United States enacted an oil embargo against the Japanese, as did Britain. Japan wanted recognition of its new expanded authority in Asia, but the Allies called on Japan to cease hostilities and withdraw from China. The Japanese made an attempt at a settlement with the United States in November 1941, but the Secretary of State was unable to accept certain provisions in the agreement. The United States would not give in to Japan's political or trade demands.

Roosevelt continued to press for peace, even as late as December 6. But the decision had already made that Japan would attack the United States. At 8 o'clock, on what had been a peaceful Sunday morning, on December 7, 1941, the full might of a Japanese naval air fleet (353 planes) struck at the Pearl Harbor base on the island of Oahu in Hawaii. The attack, a complete surprise, cost the United States heavily. More than 100 of the navy's best ships were sunk, including the battleship *Arizona* and 1,177 of her crew who were killed when a 1,500-pound (680 kg) bomb hit the ship and set off explosions and fires. A total of 3,000 Americans died and much of the navy's Pacific Fleet now lay at the bottom of the harbor. A state of emergency was declared for all of Hawaii in the chaotic hours that followed. A raid of the Japanese embassy in Honolulu found dignitaries burning important documents.

The same day as the Pearl Harbor attack, the Japanese struck elsewhere in the Pacific, attacking Malaya, Hong Kong, Guam, the Philippines, Wake Island, and Midway Island. President Roosevelt made an emergency speech to Congress and the nation on December 8: "Yesterday, December 7th, 1941—a date which will live in infamy—the United States of America was suddenly and deliberately attacked by naval and air forces of the Empire of Japan. The United States was at peace with that nation . . . and was still in conversation with the government and its

➤ **The surprise attack on Pearl Harbor, December 7, 1941.**

emperor looking toward the maintenance of peace in the Pacific. . . . As commander in chief of the army and navy, I have directed that all measures be taken for our defense."

Within a few days, war was declared between the Allies and Japan, as well as the United States and other Axis powers, Germany and Italy. Twenty-three years after the armistice of World War I, America was at war again, facing greater and more powerful enemies than ever before.

Staying Out of Harm's Reach
Musya L., born 1915

In late 1941 the Germans advanced deeper and deeper into Russia. Hard times followed for the Rus-

 # Draw a Recruiting Poster

In this activity, you will design a recruiting poster. Successful recruiting posters were designed to touch off many feelings in the average citizen, including fear, anger, patriotism, and pride. These posters often depicted symbols of national pride, or sometimes even pictures of the enemy, to inspire people to join up for military service. For an example of a patriotic illustration, look at the cover of the Defense Stamp Album in Chapter 3.

MATERIALS
✷ White card stock paper
✷ Pencil
✷ Markers

Draw some patriotic images on the center of the paper. Some possible ideas for poster images include flags, pictures of President Roosevelt, Douglas MacArthur, Dwight Eisenhower, Winston Churchill, tanks, airplanes, battleships, submarines, soldiers, guns, or the Statue of Liberty. You can also cut out pictures from magazines and newspapers or photocopy images from this book to help make your poster.

Now think of a slogan or message to write in large letters above and below the picture(s) you have drawn. Remember, the goal of these posters was to get people to enlist. Some key words to think about including are: freedom, liberty, America, fight, win, life, forever, victory, and Allies.

sians. Toward the end of September 1941 Musya's husband Joseph received a telegram signed by Stalin ordering that he be evacuated to Moscow, 400 miles (640 km) to the north and east. Under Stalin's "scorched earth" policy everything, from livestock to gasoline to wheat fields to buildings, rails, and factories, was ordered destroyed along the front lines as the Germans got close. Joseph was needed to design factories to replace those that had been destroyed.

Musya, Joseph, and their two-year-old daughter boarded the eight- or nine-car-long train at their hometown of Khar'kov, about 525 miles from Poland, in the Ukraine. The ride was uneventful until they crossed into the desolate area near Kursk, about 130 miles (210 km) north from Khar'kov. The train's passengers, many resting or sleeping, were shocked by loud blasts from just outside. A German airplane had spotted the train and was trying to destroy it with bombs. Suddenly, the train lurched to a stop in the middle of the deserted Russian steppe. Passengers panicked. Half of them left the train in a fright. Some rushed off the train, others carried their children off the train. In the chaos mothers and fathers and children became separated. In a moment that would determine their fate, Musya and Joseph tried to decide what to do. In the end they decided to stay on the train. Musya took off her fur coat and wrapped her daughter in it and then hid the child under their berth to protect her.

Then, before they knew it, the engineer decided to go and jolted the train forward, throwing the passengers off balance. In a few seconds the train was speeding along again, faster than ever. The people who had panicked and left the train were stranded in the chilly, lonely Russian steppe. Musya imagines that they must have been easy targets for the German Luftwaffe. Musya remembers how thankful she was that they made that fateful decision to stay on the train, for not long after, all three family members arrived safely in Moscow.

Musya remembers the barrage balloons floating over Moscow. People had to put black fabric over their windows. Every neighborhood had a public address system mounted to light poles. Every time a city was occupied by the Germans or won back by the Russians, the radio announcer's voice came over the speaker. Musya was annoyed by this constant noise. Three or four times a day, everyone had to go down to the local bomb shelter because of German air raids. When the situation became desperate on October 13, all nonessential personnel were evacuated from Moscow. Musya and family were sent on a crowded train to Saratov, where they transferred to a train headed for Balakova. This city was 500 (800 km) miles to the east, far from the front. The trip took a very long time because the train was stuck behind other trains carrying weapons and other evacuees. Within a year, the Germans bombed Balakova, and Musya was sent even further away to Uzbekistan.

➤ **Musya and Joseph**

2

THE LONG ROAD AHEAD

>> **At the beginning of 1942, things looked dismal for the Allies. Hitler's army had overrun most of Europe. England had successfully defended herself against German air attack, but there was no guarantee that the Germans would not attack again, or even try to invade Britain in the future. There was also no immediate hope of the Allies crossing the English Channel and invading France. Across the Mediterranean the Germans were**

☆ ☆ ☆ ☆ ☆ ☆ ☆ ☆ ☆ ☆

threatening most of North Africa. By 1942, the German war effort was in Africa, Western Europe, Eastern Europe, and the Soviet Union. All able-bodied Germans were put to work for the war effort. They built roads and made everything from guns to medical cotton.

On the other side of the world the Japanese had already made significant advances in the Pacific. People wondered how America could defeat two enemies across several continents without suffering tremendous hardships. In early 1942, the war effort appeared to be a long road ahead. Because American war factories were not yet in full production, early soldiers trained with old equipment. The draft enacted by the government was just beginning, so the armed forces had not yet grown to the millions of people who would be fighting by the end of the war.

✉ The first few days of work are behind me, first with one of the machines and now I have to take care of two machines. They are pretty big and one has to walk from one to the other and I have to put cotton into one for medical cotton and for cigarette filters in the other one.... Anyhow, I'm one of the workers inhaling cotton dust. So I do heavy work and that is no joke, and I get food coupons. And it is also very warm.

I and all the others take off our dresses and just wear the coat. Then the machines are started and shut down and in the end they get oiled and I have to get on top and open up the valves, and at the end of the day we have to sweep the room. .... Anyhow, I cannot complain. Thomasi is worse off, she deals with rags which have been dry cleaned, but are very dusty.... Next week I will be at other machines, which are even bigger than these. I'm doing well and really proud that no cotton fell off.

Letter from Frieda to her mother

July 25, 1941, Germany

Japanese Victories in the Pacific

While the United States still reeled from the surprise attack on Pearl Harbor, it seemed like the Japanese were everywhere. They began a rapid assault on a series of large southeast Asian countries, and they attacked a number of small but strategic islands dotting across the South Pacific. The Japanese captured Wake Island on December 24, 1941. On Christmas Day, the island of Hong Kong surrendered. Malaya fell next. On February 15, 1942, Singapore Island fell, resulting in the capture of more than 60,000 Indian, British, and Australian troops. Rangoon, Burma, fell on March 20. Suddenly the Japanese were within striking distance of India. The Philippines was also in danger as 57,000 Japanese troops poured into the country. American General Douglas MacArthur and his men fought bravely in the Philippines, but the Japanese pushed American troops until they were trapped in a place called the Bataan peninsula.

Unwilling to lose one of his brightest stars, in March President Roosevelt called MacArthur back from the Philippines. "I shall return," MacArthur said famously as he left the embattled remnants of his army to continue fighting under General Jonathan Wainwright. Hunger and disease took their toll, and the constant shellfire from the Japanese was devastating. On May 6, Wainwright surrendered to the Japanese. What followed was the infamous Bataan Death March. The Japanese forced weak and dying soldiers to march 60 miles (100 km) under the hot sun. The soldiers either died or were killed when they stopped to rest. Thousands did not make it.

In the spring of 1942, the outlook in the Pacific was bleak for the Allies. On the evening of June 3, the Japanese bombed Dutch Harbor, Alaska. They killed 43, but caused only minor damage. Americans now feared an attack on the continental United States. The president knew that unlike the European war, this war would have to be fought and won mostly by the navy and marines. In April, air raids on Tokyo and six other Japanese cities proved successful. But the United States would have to gain some ground in the Pacific to free shipping lanes and to create a nearby base of operations for future attacks.

➤ Sixty American soldiers with gear and helmets stand at attention during a drill.

➤ Page from a wartime Japanese schoolbook printed in 1941. Called the *Book of Numbers*, it taught children how to count using planes and warships.

The first major victories for the Allies came at the Battle of Coral Sea in May and the more important Battle of Midway Island in June. At these battles, the invading Japanese navy was stunned by the American dive-bombers. The Japanese watched in horror as several of their ships were seriously damaged, and the flaming wrecks of three aircraft carriers sank with all their planes.

By the summer of 1942, Americans were hopeful for more victories but very aware of the difficult fight that lay ahead of them in the Pacific. To defeat Japan, the United States would not only have to win back all the South Pacific islands taken by the Japanese, they would have to return to the Philippines and possibly invade Japan itself.

Meanwhile, on the West Coast of the United States, thousands of Japanese Americans were forcibly sent to fenced-in internment camps. The government thought they might be a threat to national security. These "threats," including women, children, and the elderly, were forced to spend much of the war away from civilization. Orders were issued on April 1, 1942, giving Japanese Americans six days to pack up personal items, including sheets and pillows, clothing, silverware, and dishes. Larger items such as pianos and furniture would be placed in storage. Over the course of the war, a total of 120,000 Japanese Americans were held in camps against their will.

The Four Corners of the Globe

World War II was truly a world war fought by millions of people from dozens of countries across the globe. Though not always on the front pages of the newspapers, faraway struggles were still crucial in determining who would win the war. Some of the most far-flung outposts of the world were key places during the war. In these places it really mattered who controlled the territory. Highlighted below are just a few of the war's outposts.

The Caribbean and Central America

As part of the deal made with Churchill in September 1940, the United States received 99-year leases on British bases in the Bahamas, Jamaica, St. Lucia, Antigua, Trinidad, and British Guiana. There were also about 28,000 American troops stationed at the Panama Canal Zone to prevent the Germans from getting control of the important canal waterway.

Greenland

In November 1940, Denmark asked the United States to help protect her large but sparsely populated island territory of Greenland. The U.S. Coast Guard helped rescue downed Allied planes, protect Allied weather stations, and find and destroy German weather stations. This was done with the help of the native Greenland population, who were very familiar with the features of the rugged land.

Alaska and the Aleutian Islands

The islands of Attu and Kiska were part of a long chain of islands off the coast of Alaska called the Aleutians. Both islands were invaded by the Japanese in June 1942. For many months, the United States planned an attack. Finally, on May 11, 1943, 11,000 American troops landed on Attu and had to contend with extremely foggy and windy conditions. In the 20-day battle that followed, more than 2,000 Japanese and 500 Americans were killed. In August 1943, when 34,000 American troops invaded Kiska, it was discovered that the Japanese had already abandoned the island after the costly defeat at Attu.

Because of the Japanese threat to mainland Alaska, thousands of troops were stationed at various bases around the territory. War planes patrolled the territory while ground troops were trained in winter warfare. The 1,600-mile-long (2,600 km) Alaska-Canada highway, also known as "Alcan," was built during the war as a way of

➤ **Royal Canadian Air Force (RCAF) Kittyhawk planes patrol the skies near Alaska.**

GOOSE BAY AIR BASE
CANADIAN-BUILT OUTPOST IS ONE OF THE WORLDS LARGEST AND MOST IMPORTANT. HERE, ARMY MEN ARE TRAINED IN WINTER WARFARE.

➤ **Training Allied soldiers with early pattern anti-tank rifles in winter warfare at the Goose Bay Air Base in Canada.**

making sure that supplies and soldiers could get to Alaska easily and quickly from the continental United States via the city of Edmonton, Alberta, in Canada. About 40,000 Americans helped build this highway in sometimes frigid conditions.

Iraq and Syria

The British seized control of Iraq in May 1941 because they wanted to strike at Axis-held Syria. The country was important because it could allow the Germans to build up enough strength to invade the entire Middle East. Allied forces, which included many French resistance soldiers, known as the Free French, had to face 35,000 Axis French soldiers, known as the Vichy French for the Nazi-sympathetic government that ran France from the city of Vichy. On June 8, 1942, the Allied forces attacked Syria, and on June 21 they took the capital city of Damascus. Over 1,000 people died on each side in the fighting for Syria.

Burma

The Japanese advanced from Thailand into Burma in January 1942. The capital city of Rangoon fell to the Japanese on March 20. The Allies took this very seriously because it was a threat to the British-controlled subcontinent of India. Three British-Indian divisions fought the Japanese in the jungles, but retreat was the only option for the outmatched British troops. Many troops were lost during the nearly 1,000-mile (1,600 km) retreat through treacherous terrain. They battled both the Japanese and the terrain— sultry, steamy jungles and arid plains, raging rivers and rough mountains. During the monsoon season, the torrential rain could cause deadly floods. As the British retreated, they set fire to thousands of oil wells to temporarily prevent the Japanese from using them as a fuel source.

➤ A U.S. soldier's snapshot of President Roosevelt seated in a jeep, possibly taken in North Africa.

It would be another two years before the Allies were able to make any significant progress and finally recapture Burma. In the meantime, the British and other Allied soldiers tried to fortify India to prevent any further advances by the Japanese.

The Arctic

The shipping of deliveries to Russia from America had to go by way of Arctic waters, within 300 miles (480 km) of the Arctic Circle. It was a dangerous journey because of the close proximity to German ships and submarines. Convoy PQ 13 lost 5 ships out of 19 in April 1942, and other convoys fared no better. The British destroyer *Edinburgh* was badly damaged by a German submarine. In May, Stalin wrote impatiently to Churchill that 90 ships were stuck at Iceland, waiting to sail to Russia with important war supplies. Churchill replied that he would do the best he could.

On June 27, 1942, convoy PQ 17 left Iceland for Russia with 34 merchant ships and a naval

➤ This map shows the location of hidden Allied food and supplies in the area of the newly built Ledo Road in Burma. The road was constructed by the U.S. Army Corps of Engineers to help create a supply route from India to China.

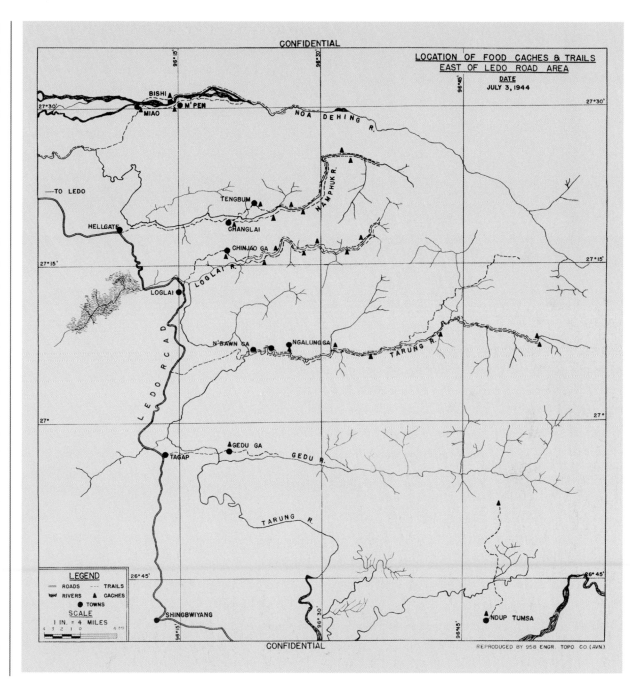

escort. Forced by ice floes to pass too far south, near German air bases, the convoy was spotted on July 1. The decision was made to have the naval escort retreat toward the west as quickly as possible and have the ships of the merchant convoy scatter and seek shelter at the nearest ports. It proved to be a disastrous decision for the defenseless ships, because the Germans sank 23 of the 34 ships.

In the aftermath Stalin still argued for continuation of shipments. He stated that in wartime no important effort could be undertaken without risks or losses. The Allies were reluctant to send more convoys because the cost was too high. If too many naval escort ships were sunk it would be impossible to defend the North Atlantic. Hitler's U-boats would rule the seas and prevent any Allied supplies from crossing the

 # Break the Code

Getting a message from one person to another many miles away often involved translating the message into an agreed-upon code so the enemy could not steal information. One of the greatest Allied challenges of the war was to crack the German "Enigma" code. The Enigma was a special machine with settings that could be changed to create an infinite number of different scrambles. The machine operator at the receiving station knew the exact code to enter in order to decode the message. To anyone else the jumble would be meaningless. The code was finally cracked after some of the machines were stolen and thoroughly examined.

In this activity, you will create a code with a friend and see if anyone can crack it.

MATERIALS

☆ Pen
☆ Paper

The Enigma machine was unique. It created an infinite variety of random codes. Most codes used in the military had some logical or numerical basis. Write out this code key:

Take the letters of the alphabet and assign each one a number beginning with A = 1, B = 2, etc. For the first five numbers, add 28, so A = 29 (1 + 28), B = 30 (2 + 28), etc. For the next five numbers, add 38, so F = 44 (6 + 38), G = 45 (7 + 38), etc. For the next five numbers, add 48, so that K = 59 (11 + 48), L = 60 (12 + 48). For the five after that, add 58, so P =

74 (16 + 58), Q = 75 (17 + 58), etc. For the next five, add 68, so that U = 89 (21 + 68), V = 90 (22 + 68), etc. For the letter Z add 78 so that Z = 104 (26 + 78). Use a hyphen between words.

As practice, decode this message:

61 33 33 78 – 61 33 – 60 29 78 33 76

Write out a one- or two-sentence-long message to a friend. Now translate it into a numerical-based code using the key. Give your friend both the coded message and the original sentence in English. Tell him or her to figure out the coding system based on this information alone.

Next, come up with your own code.

ANSWER: Meet me later

ocean. While it lasted, the convoy program succeeded in delivering 3,000 tanks, 2,500 planes, and 600,000 tons of ammunition to Russia, though more than 1,000 tanks and 600 planes were sent to their icy graves at the bottom of the sea after their ships were sunk by the Germans.

The Siege of Stalingrad

After the difficult winter of 1941–1942, the Germans regrouped and began a new offensive. They pushed farther inland, this time toward the cities of Stalingrad, Moscow, and Leningrad. Hitler felt that defeat at these three locations might be enough to cause the Soviet Union to surrender. In July 1942, Stalin ordered his army never to retreat in battle. He stated that the only choices were "victory or death."

By August 19, 1942, German forces under the command of General Friedrich von Paulus (1890–1957) were within striking distance of Stalingrad, a key tank manufacturing city located on the Volga River. By the end of that month, the siege of Stalingrad began. It was a terrible time for the citizens of the city, most of whom fled in terror. It was also a terrible time for the Germans. Soviet resistance was strong, and anti-tank detachments fired on the advanc-

С новым годом, товарищ фронтовик! В 1942 году желаем тебе новых подвигов, новой славы и полной победы над врагом. Смерть немецким оккупантам!

ing enemy. In October, rain and mud slowed the Germans. Still, by November the Germans had pierced through the some of the city's defenses. Army chaplains gave their blessings to the German soldiers who were about to enter the war zone, many never to return home. Germans who had advanced into Stalingrad took shelter wherever they could, including abandoned and bombed out buildings. House to house fighting took place. Soviet soldiers positioned in strategic locations within the ruined city fired on the Germans. With pinpoint accuracy, one Russian sniper alone killed more than 200 Germans.

➤ Russian stationery that says, "Happy New Year, front line comrade. In 1942, wishing you new heroics, new fame, and total victory over the enemy. Death to the Nazi invaders!"

➤ German vehicles had to contend with mud and snow during their invasion.

On November 23, General Paulus wrote to Hitler telling him that supplies and ammunition were quickly running out. He urged a retreat to regroup and concentrate the German forces for a fresh attack. But Hitler was not willing to abandon so much material.

Luckily for the Russians it was now the beginning of another icy cold winter. The Russians, under Marshal Georgi Zhukov (1896–1974), closed in around the German army in a pincers movement that cut off their line of supply from the west, a line already slowed by the snow and mud. A total of 250,000 German troops were surrounded. By January 31, 1942, the German Army at Stalingrad was completely destroyed, with 95,000 killed and more than 70,000 captured. Only about 5,000 of the prisoners survived. On February 2, against Hitler's wishes,

General Paulus saw no choice but to surrender. The defeat marked the turning point in Germany's attack on Russia and the beginning of the end of their success in the east.

The Germans Versus the Russians
Corporal Willy H., born 1923

In 1941, when Willy was seventeen, he was recruited for the *Arbeitsdienst* (work service). First he traveled to Frankfurt. From there he had to go to Chartreuse in occupied France where he sorted and cleaned ammunition. After nine months, he had two weeks furlough. Then he was recruited for military service and traveled to the Thuringia region of Germany for combat training. He was sent to southern France, and then in 1942 to Russia in a motorized division. He spent time near Stalino, now called Donetsk, in the Ukraine.

In the Ukraine, the soldiers had almost no time to relax or wash themselves. Willy could always hear the bullets that flew through the air and the bombs that exploded somewhere in the distance. When soldiers first arrived at a new location they had to dig a trench where they could hide themselves so they wouldn't be seen by the enemy. They were even in the trenches during the cold Soviet winter. Many soldiers froze to death in these holes.

Willy had a little tin box with a hole in it. He made a fire inside the box for a little warmth. When he came out of the trench, his face and clothing were black from the smoke.

Once someone told him that a good friend of his was killed. Willy and another friend decided to get him. They rode a tank to retreive the body. One half of his friend's head had been blown away.

Conditions on the front were so bad that to escape some soldiers even tried to fall asleep in the snow so they would become ill. Others tried to freeze parts of their bodies so they would be sent home, but it didn't work.

Once Willy had to help guard a food storehouse. He said that this was the best time for him because not much happened there. In the warehouse there were barrels containing frozen olive oil. Willy had the idea to scratch some of the oil from a little hole in the bottom, so you couldn't see anything was missing when the barrel was opened. The soldiers ate some of the oil and traded some for food.

While in Russia Willy met a local fortune-teller who wanted to look at his hand. She said she could tell his future. The fortune-teller told him that he would return home safely, and she was right.

Struggles in Africa

Though the early Axis victories in the deserts of North Africa were making the Allied leaders nervous, in 1942 they were optimistic about the African front. Mussolini's invasion of Ethiopia was squashed by the British in March 1941, but Hitler soon sent reinforcements to Africa. These reinforcements grew into what became known as the Afrika Korps, led by General Erwin Rommel. The newly fortified Axis army in Africa was now regrouped in the North Sahara desert near the Mediterranean, pushing toward Egypt and the very important Suez Canal. To repel the Axis advances the British amassed an army consisting of English, Indians, Australians, and New Zealanders.

In mid-June 1942 Rommel rolled through El Adem, Belhamed, and Acroma in Libya within the space of a few days. He had momentum and was heading toward the Allied stronghold city of Tobruk, also in Libya. On June 20, using planes and tanks, Rommel opened his offensive on the city. The resulting firestorm ended in the surrender of 35,000 British troops, a major defeat for the British. The newly promoted Field Marshal Rommel pushed his men hard through the barren landscape toward the border of Egypt. Near El Alamein, Egypt, the British tried to hold back the advancing Germans during the summer months of 1942. It wasn't easy. The Germans used tanks called Panzers with heavy armor and great firepower. They were well suited for battles in the desert.

America was eager to help the Allies in their fight against Rommel's forces. In July, President

Bazooka

The introduction of a new gun called the "bazooka" helped the Americans gain momentum in Africa. This hand-held gun could fire a 3.4 pound (1.5 kg) rocket capable of penetrating armor, brick, or stone. The shell was a true rocket because it had fins to stabilize it in flight and fuel to burn as it flew. The shooter knelt while the loader placed the rocket in the tube. The bazooka also played a part in the Russian victory at Kursk in 1943.

➤ A bazooka-man cuts loose at an enemy machine gun nest 300 yards away.

➤ Famed war correspondent Ernie Pyle wrote that Italian prisoners seemed "relieved" and "friendly." This photo shows prisoners on the road to Bizerte, Tunisia.

Roosevelt sent about 65 heavy bombers to help in the defense of Egypt. Rommel's attack was held back for the moment as he regrouped.

Churchill wanted another big attack, but the British General Montgomery wanted to spend a few weeks to build up his manpower and supplies. The wait paid off. On the night of October 23, 1942, the Allies hit hard. Within less than two weeks, Rommel ordered his men to withdraw after having suffered heavy losses. The Axis minefields and anti-tank guns caused the Allies to lose 13,000 men; still, the British were able to capture 20,000 enemy soldiers. The victory was important enough that Churchill considered having bells rung throughout England for the first time during the war to proclaim a key victory.

American and British troops landed on the shores of Northern Africa and in key inland locations by parachute in November of 1942. Called "Operation Torch," the offensive created a much stronger Allied presence. Even with more than 100,000 American troops landing, only 360 men were killed. This early success was deceiving. Soon after, when the Allies engaged the German main force, losses were heavy.

Meanwhile, the British continued to make progress. By the time the Americans landed in November, the British had already destroyed 500 German tanks and taken a total of almost 40,000 men prisoner. Still, in a radio speech, Hitler said Germany could not and would not compromise, but would keep fighting.

Around this time President Roosevelt recognized that the situation in Africa and the rest of the world would require more manpower. He lowered the minimum draft age, ordering the registration to extend to any male having reached 18 years of age. This move would allow an additional 500,000 men to be called up for service.

In December 1942, the German army was able to rebuild from a base in Tunisia. They soon numbered 50,000. Once again, the Allies were worried. They planned an attack on the city of Tunis in the spring of 1943. Bombing of Axis transport planes and ships helped the Allies to victory. On May 10, 1943, the headlines of the Stars and Stripes newspaper screamed "50,000 Prisoners Captured." By May 13, it was all over. In the space of one week, 150,000 prisoners were taken, for a total of 400,000 Axis prisoners in the African Campaign.

The successful naval invasion and teamwork of the Americans and British set the stage for future successes. Most importantly, it showed the Allies that with American help the Germans could be outnumbered. Even with their superior tanks and firepower, the German soldiers were growing tired. Fresh American troops fueled hopes of an Allied victory. An African foothold was key to success in Europe.

Surrender Propaganda

All the major players in the war used propaganda against their enemies, taking facts and rearranging them to intimidate or convince the enemy to surrender. Here are actual excerpts from Russian and German propaganda leaflets of the time. These were designed to be effective against the homesick Germans who had suffered through one or more frigid Russian winters and against the Russians who saw their homeland overrun by Germans.

RUSSIAN PROPAGANDA

In one leaflet, a German prisoner is quoted as saying: "We were told that the war would last two to three months and then we would return home. It's been more than seven months and the end of the war is not in sight. Every day friends and acquaintances die. Why should we risk our necks?" Another flyer quoted a prisoner as saying: "The days are spent in peaceful work. . . . We saw the film *Parade of Youth* of sports in the Soviet Union. On Sunday, April 5, we held a concert. . . . There were Russian melodies and German folk songs. . . . The time since we were brought here is not wasted. We read much and learn much. We are free from the nightmare of the war."

On most propaganda flyers, the following was printed in Russian and German, so Russian officers could understand it: "With this pass, every German soldier has the right to cross the front line to be taken as a Russian prisoner. . . . The Russian army guarantees the prisoner his life, good treatment, and return home after the war."

GERMAN PROPAGANDA

One leaflet printed by the Germans in Russian told Russian soldiers not to believe the lies their superiors were telling them about the Germans and about Russian prisoners of war being tortured and then killed. "The truth is on our side. See the picture that gives an answer to the gossip," the leaflet said, asking the reader to look at the photo of clean-cut, healthy looking Russian prisoners.

The harsh reality of the war was that both German and Russian prisoners had a rough time and a very poor survival rate. This is especially true for the Russian prisoners, of whom more than 3,000,000 were estimated to have died in captivity.

➤ Quoting numbers of captured men, these propaganda leaflets were distributed by Russians to German troops.

Camouflage Activity

The front lines of the war in Western Europe were sometimes in areas of heavy vegetation and dense forests. Vehicles and weapons needed to be camouflaged so that the enemy could not spot them as easily. The photo at the right shows a German vehicle hidden in a French forest. In this game, you will try to camouflage a bicycle so your friend has trouble seeing it from a distance.

MATERIALS

* Bicycle
* Camera and film
* Binoculars
* Tree branches, twigs, leaves (Ask an adult to get some for you; hedge clippings can be used as well)

Bring your bicycle to a place where there are shrubs, leaves, or trees in the background. Tell your friend to take the camera and binoculars and go at least 75 to 100 feet (23 to 30 m) away, more if possible. Have your friend photograph your bicycle from a distance before it is camouflaged. Use the twigs and tree branches to cover your bicycle, making sure you place branches in the spokes of the wheels. Have your friend look through the binoculars and see how well you have hidden your bicycle. Now have him or her take a few surveillance photographs from a distance. When the photos are developed, see how good a job you have done.

➤ A well-camouflaged German vehicle in the forest.

American Troops Amass in England

Roosevelt and Churchill met in Africa at the Casablanca Conference in Morocco in January 1943. There, the agenda for the war in 1943 was set. Among the Allies' goals was the taking of Sicily and the assembly of a huge force of troops in England in advance of an invasion of France. The powers agreed that nothing less than the "unconditional surrender" of the Axis would be accepted.

Hundreds of thousands of American soldiers streamed into the British Isles in preparation for the attack on mainland Europe. There they were set up in numerous camps across the countryside. For many of these soldiers it was their first time on foreign soil.

✉ Finally I am getting around to dropping you a line. Sometimes the Army allows for very little spare time. So far everything is going quite smoothly for us down here.... Our food has steadily been improving and along with it our general morale. It appears that soon we may be making the big trip. But just when no one knows.

George H., Camp Forrest, Tennessee

September 27, 1943

Army life was not always filled with the excitement and commotion of battle. When troops were in training or were encamped at one place for a long time, ordinary chores had to get done also, just as in civilian life.

I just got back from chow and it wasn't very good, that is I didn't care much for it. Of course you know how funny I am when it comes to eating. I hate to think about going back to our area and start in on my laundry because I have such a big one to do. Oh me! Such is life for us poor GI Joe's (a term for the average soldier, from the military production phrase "General Issue," with Joe being a slang for the average guy). I think they might send some WAACs over here to make our beds and do our laundry. Don't you think that would be a good idea? I think I'll have to sign off for now as I really have to get busy on that laundry.

Ernie M., 386th Bomb Group

July 14, 1943

Air Raids over Germany

Helga S., born 1929

"In 1940, Allied bombers were able to fly from Britain to Berlin, and Bremen was right in the flight path. That's when the alarms started, sometimes during the day, sometimes at night. The city had built air raid shelters, big concrete bunkers, half underground, in all the neighborhoods, and when the sirens wailed, we were to grab a prepared bag with the most precious possessions and hurry with everybody else towards the bunker. Inside were long corridors on several levels with wooden benches along the wall. It was either ice cold or very hot and always smelly and crowded and sometimes you had to sit for hours and hours. Neighbors tried to sit together.

"All around the city there were anti-aircraft guns trying to shoot down the bombers, so you heard those guns and bombs hitting the ground near or far. A nearby explosion took away your breath. But you knew if you heard a bomb falling, it did not hit you. What was most frightening was the noise of an approaching bomber formation, an unending deep rumble. On the 'all clear' we could go home. There the radio was on and the program got interrupted with an announcement that 'a formation of 50 bombers is approaching Groningen flying east' and you knew the alarm would come. On some nights with a clear sky we children were allowed to stay up. The parents played board games with us until the time came to leave for the air raid shelter.

Organization of the Army

A successful army is all about teamwork and chain of command. While large armies were commanded by great leaders such as Patton and MacArthur, soldiers looked to their immediate superiors for guidance. These superiors reported to their superiors, and so forth up the ladder of command all the way to the top. The branch of United States military known as "the army" actually consisted of several large fighting forces known as armies. For example, in Europe 1945 there were the United States First, Third, Seventh, and Ninth Armies. Here is the breakdown of the United States Armies of World War II:

Each army was made up of at least 2 corps.

Each corps was made up of 2 or more divisions.

Each division (about 14,000 men) was made up of several brigades or regiments.

Each brigade or regiment (about 3,000 men) contained about 3 battalions.

A battalion (about 900 men) contained 4 to 6 companies.

A company (about 100 to 200 men) was made up of several platoons.

A platoon (about 30 to 50 men) was made up of several squads.

A squad (about 10 men) was the smallest unit in the army.

➤ Patches worn on soldiers' uniforms representing the groups they were attached to. Top row, from left to right: 2nd Army, 9th Corps, 36th Corps. Middle row, left to right: 28th Infantry Division "Keystone," 86th Infantry Division, 88th Infantry Division "Blue Devils," 97th Infantry Division. Bottom row, left to right: Army Air Force Weather Specialist, Army Air Force Mechanic

"Soon many parents decided to send the children to friends or relatives in the rural areas, which were seldom bombed, and there we would be enrolled in the local school. My brother and I spent more than a year in the nearby mountains. Mother came by train to visit us on our birthdays and we got home for vacations. But I was very homesick and worried about my parents. So we both came back home, but only for a short time.

"During the school year 1942–1943 almost all schools in the city of Bremen were closed and relocated with the teachers to smaller towns and strangers took in the kids. My middle school, Vietor-Schule, went to Aue in Saxony, a pretty little town and I was again in class with my old friends and familiar teachers. But my brother's school went to a farm community about 100 miles (160 km) from where I was. I lived with a very old couple in a very old house. They were very nice and played mah-jong with me at night especially when the news said there were air raids and I was sick with worry."

Wartime Medical Treatment

During the American Civil War, modern medical care was not yet available. Many men died of their injuries or of infections that set in not

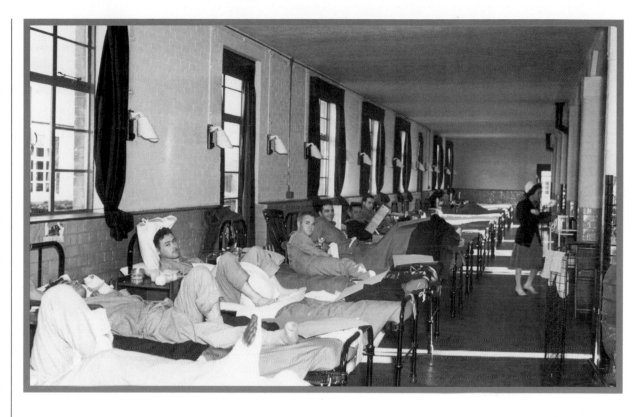

► The 65th General Hospital in England, 1943.

long afterward. By World War II, new medicines and painkillers helped soldiers on their way to recovery.

With hundreds of thousands of American soldiers wounded during World War II, medical care was crucial. As part of his field equipment, each soldier carried a very basic first aid pouch containing disinfectant and gauze at a minimum. On the battlefront, thousands of medically trained soldiers known as medics were a vital part of the war effort. When someone was injured, cries of "Medic!" rang out and the nearest medic raced to the scene. Though they were not doctors, these medics were better equipped than ordinary soldiers to handle injuries.

Even better trained were the 59,000 nurses who helped treat the injured and care for them on a long-term basis. These nurses were sent all around the world, wherever the war was raging. They landed with the Allied invasion force in North Africa in November 1942 and in France a few days after D-Day in June 1944. Doctors and surgeons were also sent overseas to treat the most difficult cases.

Medics helped stabilize the patient's condition at the battlefront until he could be moved, or at least helped by giving something to ease the pain. Not too far from the front lines of battle, field hospitals were set up, often in tents. If a soldier required further treatment or a long period of recuperation, he was taken to an evacuation hospital located farther from the battle lines. Nurses tried to stabilize their more serious patients in the field hospital to help them survive until they arrived at the evacuation hospital. For the first time ever in a war, injured soldiers were sometimes removed by airplane and flown to the nearest hospital. The most severely injured patients and those who required special care were sent to station hospitals often located in cities or towns in abandoned schools or factories. More like a regular hospital, the most permanent treatment centers were general hospitals,

where there were medical experts available to treat the most complicated injuries and illnesses.

Though hospitals were not located on the battlefront, there was still danger from snipers and air attacks, especially if the enemy could not tell from above that there was a hospital below. A white flag with a red cross helped identify a building or group of tents as a hospital facility.

Where rail systems were still intact, hospital trains were used to move patients. Special hospital ships were only allowed to carry injured military personnel, nurses, and doctors. International law stated that enemy personnel were allowed to board and inspect the ships to make sure they were not carrying any cargo.

At first, hospitals were set up in England where the American troops were amassing. After D-Day medical operations moved into continental Europe. At one point, there was fear that the Germans were going to use biological warfare. There was some talk of getting German blood samples from German prisoners of war to see what antidote the German government had given its soldiers. It was thought this procedure would allow the Allies to identify the microbe the Germans were planning to use.

✉ The hospital closed a couple of days ago and slowly but surely we are getting rid of all our patients so no doubt before long we will be seeing some different hillside or cow pasture.

1st Lieutenant Mary Catherine M.

March 14, 1945, 13th Field Hospital, Germany

Field hospitals had to follow the action and so were moved quite often, especially if a counterattack occurred and the enemy gained ground, or if things were going well and the front line was moving rapidly.

The man in charge of medical operations in Europe was Major General Paul Hawley. His title was Chief Surgeon of the European Theater of Operations. His job was to oversee the operation of the hospitals and medical treatment of the Americans who were injured in Europe. He wrote in February 1945: "[I believe that] the motive that prompts every action of this office is that of giving the best medical service to our soldiers."

 # Make a Bandage

While in many ways treatment was better than during the Civil War, some injuries were treated with measures similar to those used 80 years earlier. In the activity below you will learn to make a bandage according to a Red Cross book from 1940.

First aid on the battlefield could mean the difference between life and death. Stabilizing an injury and reducing bleeding was important because they could save a life until a soldier could be transferred to a nearby field hospital. Though the early twentieth century saw many advances in medicine and first aid, some of the basics still remained the same. In this activity, taken from a first aid handbook of the period, you will learn how to make a head bandage to hold a compress in place.

MATERIALS
* Sheet of cotton or similar type cloth, measuring 36 inches (90 cm)
* Gauze square or compress (a cotton ball will also do)
* Scissors
* Ruler
* A friend

Cut the cloth diagonally, so you have two triangles. Fold the long edge of the triangle up about 1 to 2 inches (2.5 to 5 cm) so you have a border, also known as a hem. Have your friend hold the cotton compress in place on his or her forehead. Place the bandage around your friend's head, going above the ears, so the hem is just above the eyebrows and the pointy ends of the cloth triangle are in the back. The ends will be very long, so you can wrap them back around and tie them in the front, at the center of the forehead.

Simple bandages like this were used to keep a compress against a head wound. For real injuries, sterile bandages are important to keep the wound from becoming infected.

3

THE HOME FRONT AND LIFE DURING THE WAR

>> The millions of servicemen who were drafted or joined the service voluntarily were not the only Americans affected by the war. These men left behind parents, grandparents, aunts, uncles, brothers, sisters, cousins, buddies, girlfriends, fiancées, wives, and sometimes children. Men who knew they would be shipping out often married their girlfriends before they left. Many of the men who served overseas were gone

★ ★ ★ ★ ★ ★ ★ ★ ★

for two and sometimes three years, not counting the time spent in training camps in the United States.

Being apart from loved ones was not easy. Parents of servicemen placed blue stars in their windows for each son they had in the service. If a son died, they placed a gold star in their window. Life at home went on as best it could with families broken apart. With telephone calls out of the question, writing letters was the only way to keep in touch. Millions of letters were written back and forth across the Atlantic and Pacific Oceans during World War II. Some soldiers and their sweethearts or parents wrote letters back and forth every day. Others did not have the time or could not find anything to say and wrote only every month. Requests to mothers, sisters, wives, and girlfriends most often included candy, cookies, or various types of clothing, especially by those soldiers who discovered that England and northern France, Belgium, Holland, and Germany were chilly in the winter. Cooking pamphlets of the time included tips on how to "send a box of cookies to a serviceman, today!" The instructions also explained how to properly wrap and seal baked goods to send overseas.

 ## Make a Care Package

Soldiers and sailors lived on the food rations they were given by the armed forces and used the clothes they were issued. Many relied heavily on parents, girlfriends, wives, or sisters to send them needed supplies as well as luxuries they could not get abroad. In this activity, you will make up a package to send to someone—either friend or family—who lives far away from you. If it is someone your age, maybe he or she can send you a package, too!

MATERIALS
* Cookies
* Candy bars
* Chewing gum
* Bar of soap
* Pair of socks
* Ballpoint pen
* Stationery
* Any other items you can think of

Find a favorite cookie recipe or two. With assistance, bake a batch of cookies. After they have cooled, carefully wrap them in plastic wrap. Get together all the other items you want to include. Try to find a box that is the right size so that the items won't rattle too much. Use newspaper as packing material to secure the items. Write a note to the person you are sending the box. Address the box and bring it to the post office. How much did it cost to mail your package?

✉ I'd appreciate your sending me some toothpaste, soap, shaving soap, razor blades. I'd also like to have a winter undershirt and several pairs of heavy socks.

Corporal Charles O.

July 4, 1944, France

✝

Will you send me some Camels ... a few bars of soap. Six packages of gum. Three pairs socks and some Milky Way bars candy. Must not weigh more than 5 pounds as they won't take it over that amount.

Private First Class Axel P.

April 1, 1945, somewhere in Europe

Air Raids and Coastal Defense

Peter P., born 1930

During the war, American coastal towns and villages would conduct air raid drills. The threat of German or Japanese planes bombing American cities was very real. After all, the Germans had bombed England for months and the Japanese had attacked Pearl Harbor. The drills were a way of keeping any invaders in the dark, so to speak, by preventing pilots from seeing their intended targets.

Peter's father worked at the Bulova watch factory in New York. During the war, Bulova shifted to the production of munitions. His father helped make ammunition for bombers. He also helped make instruments called altimeters that told pilots their airplanes' altitude and jewel bearings for the instrument panels of B-17s. Peter's father also volunteered to be an air raid warden during the war, and when the chance came, 12-year-old Peter volunteered to be an air raid messenger.

One evening every month or so, the siren at the volunteer firemen's station house would blow a signal telling the townspeople that a drill was being conducted. Everyone had to pull their shades down, shut their lights off, and stay inside. If you were in your car, you had to pull over and shut the engine and lights off. Peter's father reported to his station on a nearby street corner. The wardens had to check and make sure everyone in town was following instructions. If he found someone with their lights on, the warden would bang on the door and yell, "Hey, douse those lights!"

As messenger, Peter's job was to relay messages from one air raid post to another. He let the air raid commander know that the other stations were manned and that all was well. Then after 20 minutes or so, the signal came that the drill was over and people could turn their lights on again. These drills continued until the war ended.

➤ Peter's air raid messenger patch.

➤ A phone company advertisement asks that civilians limit their long-distance calls to keep the phone lines clear.

Rationing

Why were some foods in short supply in the United States? First, many factories that made food products had to convert at least part of their operations to making defense items. Manufacturers were simply not making as much food as they had before the war. Some food items, such as fats, were essential in making the glycerin that was an essential ingredient in explosives. Because cargo ships were vulnerable to attack by the Germans or Japanese, shipments of exotic foods that needed to cross the Atlantic or Pacific Ocean to reach the United States were limited.

One of the first things President Roosevelt did once America entered the war was to create the Office of Price Administration (OPA). Roosevelt recognized that there would have to be limits on some items. These restrictions would prevent people from buying as many of one item as they could, leaving other people with nothing. Roosevelt had earlier promised "a chicken in every pot," and he still meant it. To prevent hoarding, the government enacted rationing rules. Each person in a household was issued a ration book with specially numbered stamps inside. The ration books and design and coloring of the stamps changed with each new ration book. Ration Book One had plain stamps with numbers and no pictures. The stamps of Ration Book Three had pictures of tanks, artillery guns, and aircraft carriers. Point values for different foods were also occasionally changed by the OPA.

The Home Front During World War I, 1916–18
Ruth H., born 1902

"My father was in the Civil Defense Unit, and he patrolled the streets. My brother, 13 at the time, was a Boy Scout and he sold Liberty Bonds from a truck. My sister and I had a war garden at the Brooklyn Botanic Gardens, and we grew all kinds of vegetables. We used them for our own use and gave them to neighbors, and my mother canned a good many. And then my mother participated with a group of women who trained women to supply recipes for meatless days that were required. We had that during World War I. Sugar and meat were rationed. Children in the elementary school were taught to knit socks and scarves to send overseas to the men in service. It was a very patriotic time for people in World War I, as you can tell by the things that we did. When we got into the war, we had to give it the support that we could. On Armistice Day, I remember that my mother was in the city [New York], and the crowds were so active and excited that she was practically carried along, off her feet, by the excitement of the end of the war."

For the people who had already lived through World War I, the Second World War was yet another trying time, but the patriotic spirit on the home front was certainly nothing new, as you can tell from the above.

During the war there were a total of four different ration books issued. At first, you could not get "change" for a stamp. If something you bought was worth 7 points and you gave a 10-point stamp, that was the end of it. By the time Ration Book Four was issued, the system was perfected. Grocers were given shipments of red and blue tokens the size of a dime made of a durable material stronger than cardboard. When you spent a ration stamp, which were only good for a limited time, you could get "change" back in the ration points. These circular points did not expire and could be used at any time for canned goods (blue points) and meat, fish, and dairy items (red points). Each person had an allotment of 48 blue and 64 red points per month, not counting the spare change points that could be saved up.

On the cover of the booklet, you were supposed to write your name, address, height, weight, age, and occupation. When you wanted to buy a certain rationed food item such as sugar, meat, butter, or coffee, you had to give the merchant the ration stamps. The OPA explained which stamps were for what items and when they were to be used. When Book One was released in the spring of 1942, sugar was the only food to

be rationed. By Book Four in the summer of 1943, coffee, meat, butter, and various canned goods were included. You were only allowed to use a certain number of stamps per month, but no more. Rationing ensured that everyone in the country had a fair chance at getting hard-to-find items.

Of course, the stamps did not get you free food. They just served as your permission slip to buy a certain kind of food. Having stamps did not guarantee that there would be any rationed food left in the store. For this reason, a black market in rationed goods, including gasoline, thrived.

Wartime cookbooks and pamphlets showed Americans how to make the most of meat, cheese, and butter. They also explained how to substitute honey, molasses, and other sweeteners for sugar. Some recipes went to extremes to help households save rationed food—including such dishes as as nutburgers, eggless and butterless cake, raisin topping, and chocolate cake made with leftover bacon fat. "It is our patriotic duty to feed our families well . . . to serve nourishing food in our homes daily. So you have a real job to do in your country's defense. . . . " wrote Aunt Jenny, the spokeswoman for Spry vegetable shortening. "Food is vital wartime material. . . . At the end of the day, let us be sure we can say, I wasted no food today," wrote General Mills in a 1943 cookbook.

➤ Back cover of War Ration Book No. 4. and ration stamps from War Ration Book No. 3.

★ Grow a Victory Garden

During the war, Americans were urged to grow their own food in what were called "victory gardens" to help ease food shortages. Helping grow these gardens was one sure way kids could play a part in the war effort.

MATERIALS
* Vegetable seeds
* Gardening tools
* Scale

Plant your seeds any time in spring or summer after the last frost. Follow directions on the seed packets and be sure to water the soil. After 50 to 80 days you should begin to see the results of your hard work. For every vegetable you pick, place it on the scale before eating and jot down the weight. In the fall, after the last vegetable ripens, total up the weight of each of your crops. Write down how much you paid for each seed packet next to the total weight of the crop. Check your supermarket listings to see how much the same amount of each vegetable would have cost if you had bought it there. As you can see, not only is a victory garden fun, it also saves your family money.

Rare Food and Rationing

Jean P., born 1929

Jean's mother worked at the meat counter at the local Atlantic & Pacific (A&P) grocery store during the war. The family lived right down the street from the store, so when Jean's mother saw a truck deliver a shipment of a scarce item, she would call the house and say, "They just delivered the mayonnaise" or "The Jell-O just arrived." Thirteen-year-old Jean would scurry down the street to the store to get some, and even though she was only a few blocks away, people would already be crowding around the delivery truck. Though items like mayonnaise and gelatin were not rationed, they were still very rare.

When the family cooked rationed food like bacon or meat, they were supposed to save the grease in a can and bring it back to the butcher. The extra glycerin in fat was then used to make explosives. As an incentive, turning in salvaged fats earned you extra ration points.

Nonfood items were also rationed, especially rubber and gasoline. The rationing of rubber began not long after the bombing of Pearl Harbor in December 1941. President Roosevelt realized most of the rubber supply that the United States imported from Asia would be off limits. Rubber was so scarce that speed restrictions of 35 miles per hour (56 kph) were ordered. At lower speeds, tires would not wear out as quickly.

As another measure to help conserve rubber, cars were inspected to make sure that tires were properly inflated, to make them last longer.

Gasoline was rationed during the war in part because it would help preserve rubber tires by forcing people to drive less. (Gasoline was needed by the armed forces. By the end of 1943, the Army Air Force alone had used 2 billion gallons, or 7.5 billion liters (L), of gas!) Each family's case was evaluated, and the family was given a sticker for their windshield. For the average driver, the "A" sticker was most common. It allowed you to purchase 4 gallons (15 L) of gasoline per week. Other stickers were for ministers, doctors, members of Congress, and members of the military. These stickers allowed essential personnel to buy more than 4 gallons of gasoline per week. Try to figure out how your family could get along on 4 gallons of gas a week.

Those people who wanted to buy a new car during the war were out of luck. All consumer car production ground to a halt by February 1942 and did not resume again until late 1945. Anyone who wanted one of the relatively few model 1942 cars that were made had to make a special request.

During the war, many car manufacturers were given defense contracts by the government, making army trucks and personnel carriers, airplanes, aircraft engines, land mine detectors, radar units, machine guns, anti-aircraft artillery, binocular

★ Rationing Game

Different foods were assigned different point values. Some foods that were not rationed, such as chicken, were still hard to find. At least precious ration points did not have to be spent on them. Wartime families learned that by purchasing ground beef and mixing it with breadcrumbs to make meatloaf saved a lot of ration points. In this game you will see how your family's diet would hold up to wartime rationing.

MATERIALS

* ✶ Six or seven rolls of pennies
* ✶ Five or six rolls of nickels
* ✶ Two paper or Styrofoam cups
* ✶ Pencil and paper
* ✶ Calculator

How many people are in your family? Multiply the number of people by the 64 red points for meat and fats. Count out that number of pennies. Multiply the number of people in your family by 48 blue points for canned and prepared foods. Count out that many nickels. These will be your family's ration points for the month. Note that sugar was allotted monthly to each family based on the number of people. It could not be purchased with ordinary ration stamps. Most of us would have no problem with sugar rations. We do less baking and cooking of sweets today than dur-

ing the 1940s, when prepackaged cookies and cakes were not so readily available.

For an entire month, write down every item that your parents buy at the supermarket that appears on the list below. Make sure you note the size of the package. Now figure out how many points your family has used up. For example, if a package of beef is 2.5 pounds (1.1 kg), use your calculator to multiply the point value per pound by 2.5. Count out your ration points into the cup. Write down how many points you have left or by how many you went over the limit. Which items on the chart would your family never buy? How did your family do on the rationing system? Note that people ate more meat in the 1940s. They did more baking using sugar and butter. Rationing of these foods had a greater impact than it would today.

Rationing Chart from 1943 (First mark which foods require red points and which foods require blue points.)

_____ **Butter:** 16 points/pound

_____ **Margarine:** 4 points/pound

_____ **Beefsteak:** 12 points/pound

_____ **Ground beef:** 7 points/pound

_____ **Other cuts of beef:** 8 points/pound

_____ **Pork:** 7 points/pound

_____ **Lamb chops:** 9 points/pound

_____ **Ham:** 7 points/pound

_____ **Cheese:** 8 points/pound

_____ **Can of pineapple juice:** 22 points/46 oz.

_____ **Can of peaches:** 18 points/16 oz.

_____ **Can of carrots:** 6 points/16 oz

_____ **Can of sardines:** 12 points/16 oz.

_____ **Dried beef:** 16 points/16 oz.

_____ **Ketchup:** 14 points/bottle

_____ **Baby food:** 1 point/4.5 oz. jar

_____ **Frozen fruit juice:** 1 point/6 oz. can

_____ **Canned milk:** 1 point/16 oz.

➤ 54 points of rationed goods.

cases, and other defense machinery. One car company alone, Nash, received $600 million of defense orders. Two main companies, Ford and Willys, made the famous Jeeps that were used by the U.S. Army.

Rationing was difficult and uncomfortable for many families during the war. It affected everything from what you ate to where you went to the shoes you wore. Rubber soles made shoes a rationed item, too. Rationing of most items ended not long after the war. By freeing up precious materials for use in war related manufacturing, rationing may have made a significant contribution to the Allied victory.

 ## Butter Extender Activity

Wartime rationing was necessary to prevent hoarding and to allow all people the same amount of these shortage foods. But wartime families had tricks to substitute for the foods that were hard to find. Instead of butter, fat from meat could be saved and used for cooking and baking. One wartime cookbook urged people to "be patriotic, return any leftover fats to your butcher for wartime use!" There were many special cookbooks published during the war. Most of them had helpful hints on how to get the most from foods. Actual tips included a recipe for cooking wilted lettuce and cauliflower leaves and recipes for "Old-time Refrigerator Pudding," "Emergency Steak," "Buttered and Salted Cereal," and "Mock Apple Pie."

At 16 points per pound, butter was one of the most expensive and sought-after wartime rarities. In this activity, you will learn how wartime families could get more out of their precious butter by extending it. This recipe is adapted from an actual wartime cookbook.

MATERIALS

✳ 1 package of plain gelatin
✳ 1 lb. of butter (softened)
✳ 2 cups of milk
✳ 1 teaspoon salt
✳ Small rectangular plastic container
✳ Mixer or beater
✳ Small metal mixing bowl
✳ Large metal mixing bowl
✳ Large pot with 2 inches of near-boiling water
✳ Wooden mixing spoon

Measure 2 teaspoons of gelatin into the small pot and stir in ¼ cup of milk using the wooden spoon. Slowly place the mixing bowl into the pot with the hot water and stir until the gelatin is dissolved. Now add the remaining 1¾ cups of milk. Place the softened butter into the large mixing bowl and add the gelatin mixture and salt. Mix at slow speed until well blended. Now pour into the rectangular container and refrigerate until solid. You should have about 2 pounds worth of "extended butter" that will last about a week. Try it on bread. How does it taste compared to the real thing?

Metals were extremely scarce during the war, especially those needed to make airplanes, ships, bombs, bullets, and gun parts. The United States Mint stopped making copper cents altogether in 1943. That year it made pennies out of steel coated with zinc. You may have seen these silvery white pennies before. From 1944 to 1946 the mint made pennies out of copper again, but these pennies were created from melted spent shell casings from ammunition. Pennies today are made of 97 percent zinc and only 3 percent copper because the price of copper became too high. The metal known as nickel was also scarce during the war. From 1942 to 1945 the mint made nickels from a mixture of copper, silver, and manganese. The Office of Price Administration (OPA) encouraged people to turn in used tin cans to be recycled. Posters were printed to encourage people to recycle. One poster of the time said, "Waste helps the enemy—conserve material," showing "wasted" paper clips, pins, rubber band, and eraser laid out to form an image of Hitler's face.

The kids who grew up during the Great Depression were used to not having many things. Children didn't have many toys, nor did they have many big meals. They may have felt the effect of rationing less than adults who could remember the times before the Great Depression when most foods were both affordable and available.

➤ **Above: The versatile Willys Jeep, 1943. Right: Cartoons from a wartime pamphlet issued by the government illustrate some of the key points about ceiling prices.**

Price Controls

Besides setting up the rationing system, the OPA also set maximum prices. Price controls prevented stores from taking advantage of people's desperation and charging outrageous prices for food and other necessities. The OPA decided that the best way to freeze prices was to set a "ceiling" or maximum price that each store could charge for an item. Under the World War II price

ALWAYS LOOK for ceiling prices!

DON'T PAY MORE than the ceiling

➤ **Kids in Roanoke, Virginia, help the war effort by collecting scrap metal, October 1942.**

18, then Joe's Store could not charge more than 22¢ for three bars of soap. If Fred's Store charged 26¢ for soap in March 1942, then the store could not charge more than 26¢ for the soap during the rest of the war.

Stores were allowed to have sales and advertise bargains to compete with other stores. But they were not allowed to go even one penny higher than the ceiling price. It is estimated that the OPA saved Americans $22 billion, or $169 per person during the war, by setting price limits.

Ceiling prices were required to be posted in plain sight for most everyday items, including meat, butter, coffee, rice, aspirin, ice, clothes, diapers, soap, napkins, furniture, shovels, towels, lightbulbs, curtains, radios, and firewood. Besides following pricing rules, stores were not allowed to cheat and lower quality. If they offered Don's Brand of Superior Soap for 22¢, they could not substitute Jim's Brand of Mediocre Soap for 22¢.

People were urged to write to their local War Price and Rationing Board to report any overcharges. The Price Control Act allowed people to sue storeowners for $50 if they were charged more than the ceiling price. The OPA found 280,000 price control violations in 1943 alone.

Overall, the price control program was a big success. Its measures helped prevent inflation from gripping the United States. By also freez-

control system, each store had to set its own ceiling price using the "base" price charged in that store for an item in March 1942, before prices began to climb.

If three bars of soap cost 20¢ in Joe's Store in February 1942, 22¢ in March, 25¢ in April, and 29¢ just before the ceiling prices were set on May ing rent prices, the OPA helped keep the cost of living down for families whose main earners had left to fight the war.

President Roosevelt

Franklin Roosevelt was an immensely popular president and the only one in history to serve more than two terms. One campaign song of 1944 was titled "Let's Re-Re-Reelect Roosevelt." Not only was he responsible for helping the United States out of the Great Depression, Roosevelt was seen as a brilliant and optimistic wartime leader. His speeches raised hopes and helped inspire America to victory. Most Americans saw no reason to fix something that was not broken and voted Roosevelt in for a third and fourth term. The president died of a cerebral hemorrhage just three months after taking office in 1945.

Excerpts from Inaugural Speech
January 20, 1941
"In the face of great perils never before encountered, our strong purpose is to protect and to perpetuate the integrity of democracy. For this we muster the spirit of America and the faith of America. We do not retreat. We are not content to stand still. As Americans, we go forward, in the service of our country, by the will of God."

Excerpts from Inaugural Speech
January 20, 1945
"In the days and in the years that are to come we shall work for a just and honorable peace, a durable peace, as today we work and fight for total victory in war. We can and will achieve such a peace. . . . We have learned that we cannot live alone, at peace; that our own well-being is dependent on the well-being of other nations far away . . . we have learned to be citizens of the world, members of the human community."

Rosie the Riveter, the WACS, and the WAVES

When America went to war, women went to work in defense plants and at shipyards doing jobs that before would have been performed by men. The millions of job openings in defense could not be filled without the help of women who were motivated by their patriotism and by the good pay these defense jobs provided.

➤ Patriotic posters such as this one encouraged American women to work in the war effort.

⭐ Making Every Scrap Count

As you have read, one of the first recycling drives took place during World War II. Kids did their part by collecting scrap metal for the war effort.

MATERIALS
* Large bag or cardboard box
* Bathroom scale

Collect all empty cans around your house for a week and put them into the bag. Also look for any scrap metal you may have—paper clips, old toy cars, anything else you can find. For example, ask your parents for any old nails or screws that may be lying around the house. At the end of the week put the bag or box on the scale and see how many pounds of scrap you have collected. Now imagine if 10 million other children had collected the same amount of scrap that week. Now consider that each bomber that flew the skies weighed about 20 tons, or 40,000 pounds (18,000 kg), much of which was metal, not including the bombs the planes carried. You can see how every piece of scrap was needed.

In the city of Richmond, Virginia, the population quadrupled during the war years as thousands of women went to work in shipyards there. The government launched a successful campaign to get more women into the work force. A song titled "Rosie the Riveter" was written in 1942, and famous illustrator Norman Rockwell drew her on the cover of the *Saturday Evening Post* in 1943. The term "Rosie the Riveter" was coined because jobs such as riveting, usually seen as men's work, were now being done by women. In one Warner Brothers cartoon of the time, a female welder is complaining that if she can't find anybody to watch her baby, she won't be able to help beat the Germans and the Japanese. When she finally finds Porky Pig to help her, she is happy that she will be able to work again. World War II was the real beginning of women working outside the home.

Besides working for private companies involved in the war effort, women joined the armed forces. They joined the Women's Army Auxiliary Corps (WAACs), which later became the Women's Army Corps (WACs). Women also joined the Women Accepted for Volunteer Emergency Service (WAVES) in the navy, or the Marine Corps Women's Reserve. Many of these women worked in the states doing a variety of jobs—everything from office paperwork to important defense-related, high-tech assignments.

Nursing School and the Cadet Nurse Corps

Ruth S. Harley, born 1902 (Dean of Women at Adelphi College, New York)
Dr. Mildred Montag, born 1908 (Founder and Director of Adelphi School of Nursing, 1943–1948)

The United States was in desperate need of nurses during the war. The demand for nurses overseas meant that there would be a shortage of civilian nurses. The Adelphi School of Nursing was founded in 1943 just before a bill called the Bolton Act created a program called the Cadet Nurse Corps. The program provided a scholarship, uniform, and a $30 monthly stipend for nursing students who promised to serve wherever they were needed during the war. The students took their 2½-year cadet training at the same time they took their normal college classes. Because of this program, Adelphi and other nursing schools began to attract students from around the country. Adelphi was also one of the few colleges that allowed Japanese students held in internment camps to be admitted into the nursing program—at least 12 of them. Yoshimori and Nakimora are two names that Ruth remembers. Ruth and Mildred recall that Adelphi was one of the top cadet corps schools in the country.

✉ I got a job as assistant driver, don't know as yet what the vehicle will

```
be ambulance, jeep, or water truck or
what but whatever it is I will be out
a while and have a chance to see what
is going on outside of our little cow
pasture sphere.

1st Lieutenant Mary Catherine M.,
13th Field Hospital

March 14, 1945, Germany
```

Women in the service were not on the front lines, but a whole range of important jobs was available for them to help support the soldiers who did fight.

Wartime Entertainment and Entertainers

Entertainment in the early 1940s was just as important as it is today. Because of the metal shortage kids could not get metal wagons or toy cars, but there were still plenty of toys and games to play. Family entertainment could come from many sources, including the piano. People who could afford them before the Great Depression or who inherited them from their parents and grandparents, played for fun. They often taught their kids to play or had them take lessons.

Besides toys and games that let young people entertain themselves, there were plenty of other forms of entertainment available to the World War II generation.

Radio

Radio was an essential part of American life by 1940. Only the poorest or most isolated families did not have a radio in the 1940s. Radio was a great way for people to get updates about the war. For Americans, the first big radio event of the war was President Roosevelt's address to the nation about the Pearl Harbor bombing and the news coverage that followed.

Once America became involved in the war, American families gathered around their radio sets after dinner to listen to news flashes from the front lines. Families elsewhere around the world listened to the radio, too. In many cases the news was even more important to them with the war going on in their own countries. War correspondents were sent to Europe and Asia to cover the war firsthand. They filed their gripping reports directly from the front.

The radio was not only a source of music and news, it also served the same purpose that television serves today. There were all kinds of

➤ These two American women worked overseas for the Office of the Chief Surgeon in Paris, 1944–45.

programs on the radio—dramas, comedies, action-adventure, and children's shows. Some of the most popular radio shows were serials, or soap operas. The main characters would get into trouble or have some crisis. Then the show would end. The listener had to wait until the next week to find out what happened. Some of the favorite kids' adventure programs were the same shows young people had been listening to for much of the Great Depression, including the Lone Ranger, the Green Lantern, and Superman.

Radio programs were often broadcast from studios in front of live audiences that supplied the laughs and cheers. The radios themselves were huge, sometimes as big as modern-day televisions. They were housed in wooden cabinets, some with record players and storage space included. The wartime radio was a piece of furniture in the living room or den. When the family listened, Mom and Dad might sit next to it in their easy chairs or on the sofa, and kids might sit cross-legged on the floor in front of the radio.

Television

Television was poised to take off in popularity by 1939 when it was displayed at the World's Fair in New York City. The 1940 presidential election was the first ever to be covered on television. Things looked promising when the Federal Communications Commission (FCC) allowed commercial broadcasting to begin as of July 1, 1941. There were already more than 10,000 television sets in the United States and a growing interest in the new medium by production companies and sponsors.

However, the American entry into World War II slowed the growth of the exciting new technology to a crawl. Only a few hours a week of programming were broadcast, including an occasional musical presentation or comedy show. Almost nobody bought a television between 1942 and 1945. Television would have to wait until after the war was over to really catch on.

Hollywood and Movie Stars

As much of a treat as radio was, movies were even more exciting, especially for kids. With the Great Depression ending, Americans finally had money to spend, but many things were scarce or not available. So off everyone went to the movie theater every Saturday or Sunday to see the latest movies. Admission was about 10¢ for a double feature. Americans weren't the only people enjoying movies. In fact, until the war started, the rest of the world, including Germany and Japan, enjoyed American movies and movie stars, too.

Once America entered the war, Hollywood churned out hundreds of war-related movies,

Stage a Radio Adventure Program

Though radio programs were not visual, they featured a wide array of sound effects to give the listener the authentic feel of the scene. If you close your eyes during a good radio drama, you should be able to imagine everything. Sometimes using your imagination is much more exciting and fun than having everything already laid out for you on a screen.

MATERIALS
★ Tape recorder
★ Blank cassette tape
★ A couple of friends
★ A variety of sound props

Collect your sound props. Some possible ideas are: spoons, pencils, a glass of water, a pot, an empty cardboard box (to punch with your fist to recreate a fistfight, or to throw against a wall to imitate the sound of a body falling to the ground), a shoe and some eggshells or corn tortilla chips (to make a crunching sound), a wet sponge, a nearby door (to open and shut), paper (to crumple), two pads of Post-it notes (to strike against each other to imitate the sound of a match being lit), a bicycle horn, a bell or a handful of jingle bells, a kazoo, a pair of shoes (to pound on the floor to simulate footsteps), several inflated balloons and a pin (for gunshots), one hand hitting your other hand (to make the sound of a slap on the face), a handful of coins, and one hand punching your other hand (to recreate a fistfight).

Here are just a few ideas for characters that you could write into your script:

Private detective, head of his or her own detective agency

Junior detective, a kid just out of detective school

Policeman who does not trust private detectives

Super hero

Villain

Villain's henchman

Journalist looking for a lead on a hot crime story

Man whose mansion was robbed by villain

Woman looking for her missing husband

Narrator (you can write short commercials for real or made-up products, read by the narrator)

Now write a short script featuring some of these characters or others you have invented. Make sure you place instructions for the sound effects into the script. Assign roles in the radio play to your friends and do a rehearsal. Include commercials just before the radio program, at a break in the middle, and at the end.

A commercial may go like this:

And now a word from our sponsor. Plenti-Bubble Soap is the best soap around. If you're not feeling clean with your current soap, it's no wonder! No other soap has the Plenti-ful cleaning power that Plenti-Bubble Brand Soap has. So don't walk around feeling dirty. Try some today!

You may want to tape-record a rehearsal to see how the sound effects come out; then you can make any adjustments or corrections. When you are ready, tape the final performance and play it back for your family and friends.

WIN THE WAR BY MAKING *more!*

despite the fact that thousands of directors and film production workers joined the service. Universal Studios alone released more than 30 war-related movies between 1942 and 1943. Major stars like John Wayne appeared in patriotic American films that showed the Germans and Japanese being defeated by the American heroes. Even Sherlock Holmes appeared in three movies about Nazi terrorism, spies, and secret codes. One of the movies featured a patriotic speech written by Arthur Conan Doyle in his original story about World War I spies. "A better, stronger land will lie in the sunshine when the storm has cleared," says Basil Rathbone as Sherlock Holmes.

Kids Help the War Effort

Joan Q., born 1932

"We collected tin cans, aluminum foil, scrap metal, newspapers, old phonograph records (which were made of hard rubber; we were told they were to be melted and then used to make tires), and bacon fat, which had to be very carefully strained to be sure it was clear.

"Collecting the aluminum foil was the most fun as it offered competition among the kids. The foil came from gum wrappers and cigarette packs. It was attached to the white paper lining and had to be peeled off the paper in one piece, which was a challenge and an art. Once you had the foil you would start making a ball of it and the goal was to make the largest ball of anyone on the block. Scrap metal drives were major community activities held twice a year.

"One year there was a drive that was so successful (we completely filled a huge vacant lot) that the *Long Island Star Journal*, the local newspaper, wrote an article about our achievements and four of us had our pictures in the paper standing in the middle of all that scrap metal, which included an old barber chair, an oil tank, and an old Model-T Ford in the assortment. Sitting in the barber chair was a dummy made up to look like Adolf Hitler with one of the boys holding a huge razor at Hitler's throat."

The master of mystery Alfred Hitchcock directed the 1942 classic film *Saboteur*, about a Nazi agent who sets fire to a Los Angeles aircraft factory. Hitchcock also directed the masterful thriller *Lifeboat* in 1944, about a sinister Nazi trapped with other people on a life raft in the ocean. The winner of the Oscar for Best Picture in 1943 was the Humphrey Bogart romantic drama *Casablanca*, set in wartime North Africa.

Crowds young and old loved these movies because they lifted spirits and gave everyone hope that the horrible war would soon be over. When the enemy villains were defeated, the crowd clapped and cheered. Between the movies of a double feature, newsreels about 5 or 10 minutes long ran in the theaters. These newsreels showed planes and tanks firing their guns and updated the public on how the war was going.

Not all the movies were serious and filled with dramatic adventures. Humor was also a very important part of keeping America in good spirits. Moe, Larry, and Curly—the Three Stooges—poked fun at Hitler in several short movies, including *I'll Never Heil Again* and *You Nazty Spy*. Everything was fair game during the war, from Hitler to the shortages of food and supplies. Nylon, rubber, and various kinds of metal were among the most scarce items during the war. Bob Hope joked that President Roosevelt needed eight Secret Service agents around his car, two to guard each rubber tire. One wartime radio show had a comedy sketch about women fighting each other to get the last pair of nylon stockings in a department store. An Abbott and Costello movie ended with a scene where Costello finds a rubber-banded wad of bills. When he sees the money, he is overjoyed and exclaims "Am I lucky! Rubber, good rubber!" and tosses the money away.

Wartime Movie Star Helps Kids, Troops

Chris Costello, daughter of Lou Costello, born 1947

"My dad was an extremely generous man who loved giving to others, especially those less fortunate. Never was his generosity so well displayed as when he and Bud toured the United States in the 1940s to raise money for the building of the Lou Costello, Jr., Youth Center in East L.A. Following its opening, dad would go out and buy truckloads of baseball equipment for the kids, and on Christmas, he would dress Joe Besser [later one of the Three Stooges] up as Santa Claus and together with friends and family would truck in toys for the kids. More than anything else, he was extremely supportive of our troops. He and Bud performed on behalf of the war effort, raising a record $30 million in just three days and being honored on the steps of New York City Hall by Mayor Fiorello LaGuardia."

Comedians Bud Abbott and Lou Costello hit it big in 1941 with their first starring movie. Called *Buck Privates*, it returned $4,000,000 in box office receipts, 20 times what the movie cost to make! Abbott and Costello were the top box office attraction in the United States in 1942 and near the top for the remainder of the war years. They were famous for their slapstick routines where short and chubby Costello fell down or did wild stunts. The two comedians were also famous for their puns and word play (Abbott: Didn't you go to school, stupid? Costello: Yes, and I came out the same way.) Their fast-paced, clean comedy routines were a good way for the American public to take their minds of the troubles of the world for a couple of hours. Critics were sometimes harsh, but the public loved them. Between

Something FOR SOMEONE In the Service

➤ **Bud Abbott (right) and Lou Costello (left) up to no good in the 1941 movie called *In the Navy*. The censors objected to one scene and new footage had to be added for the film to be released.**

1940 and 1945, Abbott and Costello made 16 films, including 5 war-related movies—*Buck Privates*, *In the Navy*, *Keep 'Em Flying*, *Who Done It?*, and *Rio Rita*. They also had a popular radio comedy show from 1938 to 1949. They were so popular that it is estimated they were responsible for selling many millions of dollars of war bonds, more than anyone else.

In 1942, Abbott and Costello even launched a special round of appearances to collect enough money to buy a bomber for the U.S. government.

They collected $350,000. In 1943, during the course of an exhausting 38-day, 85-city tour, they were persuaded by a 14-year-old boy to perform in his backyard circus for 35¢. The boy tracked them down in their hotel room in Omaha, Nebraska. He told them all the money raised from the 10¢ and 15¢ admissions would be donated to the Red Cross.

During World War II, radio and movie stars hit the road to convince the American public to buy war bonds. War bonds are a way for the government to "borrow" money from people with the promise to return it with interest after 10 or more years. During World War II, the government needed all the extra money it could get to help pay for defense equipment. Defense bonds could be bought by buying stamps for 10¢ or 15¢ each. People pasted the stamps into special booklets that, when filled, could be redeemed for a $25 war bond. Movie theaters sometimes ran special promotions that gave free admission to whoever bought a bond in the theater lobby that day.

Stars also did other things to help the war effort. By 1944 paper was getting very scarce. Wartime books were printed on special extra-thin paper. Recycling was suddenly very important. Radio stars were some of the biggest donors of scrap paper to the nationwide drive that took place late in the war. Dozens of radio shows aired each week around the country. Each show needed several copies of the lengthy script, one for each of the actors. Abbott and Costello led all radio stars with a donation of 2,000 pounds (900 kg) of old scripts that represented 10 years of radio shows. The Great Gildersleeve, another comedian, donated more than 1,000 pounds of scripts. Stars were not the only ones collecting paper. Schoolchildren around the country helped too, gathering thousands of pounds of paper for recycling.

Abbott and Costello played their parts in World War II on the home front because at age 46, Abbott was too old to serve, and Costello was not eligible because of a heart condition. Still, many other able-bodied film stars and sports stars actually enlisted in the service. Clark Gable, who had played the dashing Rhett Butler in the 1939 film *Gone With the Wind*, joined the army air force. Tyrone Power, who played Zorro, and Kirk Douglas, the father of Michael Douglas, also enlisted during the war, along with many other stars. The highest ranking movie star in the service was Colonel James Stewart, who starred in the film *It's a Wonderful Life*. Stewart flew 20 bomber missions over Germany.

Other stars who did not join the service participated in the United Service Organization (USO). Created by President Roosevelt, the non-profit group provided entertainment and recreation to United States troops around the world. Entertainers donated their time to putting on

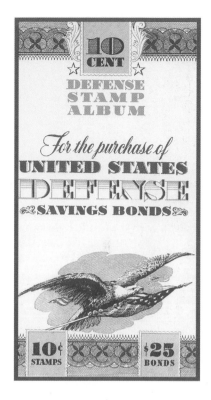

shows for troops in training camps in the United States or for troops stationed overseas. The comedian Bob Hope was the best-known and persistent USO performer. Hope performed USO shows for more than 45 years beginning in the early 1940s. Overall, the USO sponsored more than 400,000 shows for U.S. troops between 1941 and 1947!

Soldiers were lonely for their wives and girlfriends, and they missed the beautiful American movie stars they left behind. While they were stationed in training camps or in temporary

➤ A Defense Stamp Album. $18.70 of 10¢ defense stamps bought a $25 savings bond.

➤ Marlene Dietrich, seen on the cover of a 1940 Japanese magazine, entertained Allied troops with a popular version of the song "Lilli Marlene."

barracks awaiting orders, many men posted pictures of their girls or their favorite movie stars on their walls. These "pinups" were similar to what you might find in a teenager's room today, only smaller in size. The most popular pinup girl of World War II was an actress named Betty Grable. She was the top box office attraction of 1943. A photo postcard of Grable in a white swimsuit was sent to millions of American soldiers. Because of her pinup picture Grable was so popular that she had her legs insured for $1 million.

First Lady Eleanor Roosevelt

Ruth H., born 1902, and Mildred M., born 1908

Franklin Roosevelt was president longer than any other man. His wife Eleanor was the first lady longer than any other woman. Mrs. Roosevelt played an important role in keeping the country's morale high. Her seemingly endless energy led her to make public appearances on many occasions. In 1940 alone she gave more than 100 speeches around the country! The story of two people who met Mrs. Roosevelt on more than one occasion is told below.

On May 6, 1944, a crowd of thousands helped Adelphi College celebrate the opening of three new dormitories built to house the many new nursing students. The U.S. Surgeon General was present and First Lady Eleanor Roosevelt (1884–1962) was the guest speaker. Mrs. Roosevelt sat next to Ruth on the plat-

form. Ruth remembers that Mrs. Roosevelt was "a delightful woman. She was a warm person to meet." Mildred recalls taking Mrs. Roosevelt on a walking tour of the newly opened dormitories that day. She remembers that the First Lady was "very, very friendly, very kind, and very outgoing" and also most intelligent. Yet she was also modest. Said Ruth: "I was in Lord and Taylor's one time, and she [Mrs. Roosevelt] was there shopping; she was picking out handkerchiefs, and she stood in the background and never made any attempt to be recognized by the clerk. She was that simple a person at heart, and yet known as citizen of the world."

Music and Musicians

Besides actors and actresses, musicians were also an important part of the war effort. Radio stars, singers, and bandleaders participated in the USO. They crossed the country and the Atlantic Ocean to entertain the troops. The Andrews Sisters, who had also appeared in a few Abbott and Costello movies, became immensely popular with their Oscar-nominated hit song, "Boogie Woogie Bugle Boy of Company B." Bandleader and trombonist Glenn Miller entertained thousands of troops in Europe until the plane he boarded on the way to an appearance in Paris disappeared mysteriously on December 15, 1944. Jazz saxophonist and bandleader Frankie Trumbauer joined the air force and became a test pilot. He had a passion for planes and a desire to help his country. The top box office attraction from the 1940s, Bing Crosby, entertained civilians with the song "White Christmas," from the 1942 movie *Holiday Inn*. One of the most popular Christmas tunes ever, the song has sold more than 30 million copies. Crosby, who won the 1944 Academy Award for Best Actor, also entertained troops as part of the USO. His duet with the Andrews Sisters called "(There'll Be a) Hot Time in the Town of Berlin" was a top song of 1944 with its morale-boosting lyrics: "I want to be there boy, spread some joy, when they [the Americans] take old Berlin."

The song most popular with World War II soldiers was called "Lilli Marlene." Originally a German poem, it was set to music in 1938. German soldiers stationed in Africa were an enthusiastic audience. The song was soon being hummed by British and American soldiers as well. In 1944 English words were written for the tune and the song became even more popular. The German-born actress Marlene Dietrich was the most famous singer of the song. Dietrich had come to America in 1930 to act in Hollywood. She later rejected a plea by the Nazi government to return to Germany. She became an American citizen in 1939. When the war began, she did anti-Nazi broadcasts in German. Dietrich toured the Allied troops tirelessly in several countries

 # Patriotic Music

In 1942, a music publishing company in Illinois placed a magazine ad calling for songs that might be worth publishing. Over the next year more than 100 people from across the United States wrote in, some with only poems, some with words and music. While some songs were traditional tunes, many were highly patriotic. Here are some of the titles of songs that were actually submitted for publication.

It's Yanking Time (in This Old World Again) (We'll Yank Out the Japanazi)

General MacArthur—He Sure Can Fight

We're a Hundred Thirty Million Strong (and We're Going to Win This War)

We've Got to Win This War

They Can Never Take Our Freedom Away

The Yankees Are Coming Again

We're Gonna Set the Rising Sun

We Will Love America Better Than Ever Before

Lend a Hand American

Drop Your Guns You Japs

Send All Our Mail to Japan

Hello England, Here We Come

Lets Buy Bonds and Stamps and Axe the Axis

We're All with You—Oh Doug MacArthur

It's a Grand Old Flag We're Fighting For

Try to make up your own patriotic song. What would you call it? How would the tune sound? Many of these songs contain rhyming verses. Here is an example of a song's structure, consisting of verse 1, a refrain, verse 2, and the refrain repeated twice. The refrain sums up the feeling of the entire song, and is usually where the song title comes from. The refrain may have different music or a different tempo than the rest of the song.

"The Allies Can't Be Stopped"

When the ships sail swiftly in the sea,
There are men who will fight for you and me.
When the planes fly bravely in the sky,
Those are men who will fight for you and I.

Refrain: *The Allies can't be stopped.*
The Allies can't be topped.
We'll fight until we've mopped
The Axis up!

When the army marches proudly through the sand,
They'll fight for everybody in the land.
When the subs chase the enemy far below,
They'll make us very proud don't you know.

(Refrain)

(Refrain)

➤ Thousands of babies were born to women while their husbands were away in the service. Here Sergeant Jack Panchyk (the author's grandfather) visits with his newborn daughter.

during the war. She sang about the lonesome soldier who met his girlfriend Lilli Marlene "underneath the lantern by the barrack gate" until orders came to set sail, and then all he had was the memory of her standing under the glow of the lantern.

Furloughs

Furloughs are "vacation" hours or days for people in the armed forces. For those soldiers in training camps in the United States, a furlough might mean they could go home and visit with their families and friends. If home was too far away or the furlough was too short, a soldier might take in a movie or go out to dinner in the nearest town. Servicemen and women who were on leave were offered a variety of free amusements. In New York City, for example, free admissions were offered to Broadway plays and to movies at more than 10 theaters. Dances were held to raise money for the war effort.

For those who were in the service overseas, furloughs might mean taking in the sights of London or Paris or other smaller towns for a half day. The great majority of people who served in Europe or the Pacific had never left the United States before. In fact, many had never even left their home states or towns. Being in a foreign country was a strange and interesting experience

that would never be forgotten. Pocket cameras probably snapped millions of pictures of the sights in England, France, Germany, and Italy to send home. Many wartime letters told parents, sisters, brothers, girlfriends, and boyfriends of the places that were visited on leave time. Since the censors did not want them to talk about the details of the war itself, this topic was very popular.

Sports

During the 1930s and 1940s boxing was one of the biggest sports in the country. Going out to the fights was a common pastime. Americans cheered when Joe Louis defeated Hitler's pride, the German boxer Max Schmeling, to defend his heavyweight title in 1938. Boxing was still big during the war, even though several greats, including Joe Louis and another champion named Max Baer, served in the army.

Baseball stars Joe DiMaggio, Ted Williams, Bob Feller, Hank Greenberg, and Stan "the Man" Musial were among the 500 major leaguers who cut their fantastic baseball careers short to join the service. The baseball world was depleted by the war. President Roosevelt insisted that America needed baseball to continue during the war, to provide a welcome distraction from the reality of the bleak world. Many men who would not normally have had a chance to play were given major league contracts, including Pete Gray, a one-armed outfielder. Old timers who had not played in years were reactivated. Over 1,000 more fielding errors were made in 1945, than in normal prewar years. Americans didn't care. They still crowded ballparks.

Chewing gum millionaire Philip Wrigley paid for a new league of professional women's baseball in 1943. The teams helped entertain Chicago-area fans during the war. At first there were just four teams: the Peaches, Blue Sox, Belles, and Comets, but the All American Girls Baseball League (AAGBL) soon grew and drew thousands of cheering fans to games in Michigan, Illinois, Wisconsin, and Indiana. The women's league was celebrated in the 1992 movie *A League of Their Own*, starring Madonna, Tom Hanks, and Rosie O'Donnell.

Those baseball stars who did not join the service helped out by touring troop camps and signing autographs. Overseas, servicemen longing for their beloved American pastime played the game informally on makeshift fields. Because more than a million American troops were massing in England prior to the June 1944 invasion of France, Great Britain was perhaps the most popular overseas site for baseball. The British people welcomed the sport and came out to watch the strange American game that was slightly similar to their game of cricket.

While baseball was played during the war, sports in much of continental Europe came to a grinding halt. Even the Olympics were affected. Though the 1940 Olympics were scheduled to take place in Japan, that country's invasion of China caused the game site to be moved to Germany. After the invasion of Poland, the 1940 Olympics were canceled altogether. Because of the war raging in full force around much of the world, the 1944 games were not held either. At the 1948 games, neither Germany nor Japan was invited to participate.

➤ **A baseball game in England, September 1943.**

4

HOPE RENEWED

>> For the Allies, 1943 meant hope renewed. When Germany began its offensive in 1939, the country had already been manufacturing weapons and planes for six years. In short, they were armed and dangerous, more so than any other European country and far more than the United States. The German army of the late 1930s was brimming with newly trained soldiers ready for battle. Fast forward to the beginning of 1943. Now Russia,

✫ ✫ ✫ ✫ ✫ ✫ ✫ ✫ ✫ ✫

Britain, and the United States were fully immersed in the war. The draft was in full throttle, and thousands of new American soldiers were flooding into the army, navy, and marines every week. Automobile production had stopped. All available scrap metal was now being used for the manufacture of tanks, planes, guns, and ammunition. The once-fresh German soldiers were now battle-weary from their defeats in Africa and the Soviet Union. Supplies and weapons were not as plentiful as they had been, and morale in Germany was beginning to sink due to Allied bombing.

➤ **Fifth Army Invasion Training Center, Summer 1943, Oran, North Africa.**

Operation Husky

Everyone in Allied Command knew that launching an invasion of the European continent was the only way to defeat Germany. Bombing runs against Germany were proving successful, but not nearly enough to win the war. Once the Allies gained control of key parts of North Africa in early 1943, they could build up an invasion force to hop across the Mediterranean to Sicily. Because of its nearness to Italy, the island of Sicily was a key to getting the Allies into southern Europe. It was also a crucial step in clearing the Mediterranean to allow safe Allied shipping. Even better, it allowed Allied bombers a home base closer to their target—Germany. Though an invasion of France was planned, the Allies were in a better position in 1943 to invade from the Mediterranean. Besides, the Italians were vulnerable after having many soldiers captured in Africa.

The U.S. Navy had the awesome responsibility of organizing the invasion and transporting the troops, weapons, and equipment across the sea for the invasion of Sicily, code named Operation Husky. For many months, thousands of troops worked on practice landings and other maneuvers to prepare them for the largest amphibious invasion in history. When everything was set, the fleet of ships left Africa. On the night before the invasion force was due to hit the beaches of Sicily, the weather became rough with high winds and rolling waves. Many of the men became seasick. The invasion was almost postponed, but it was too late to call it off and orders were given for it to go ahead as planned.

Before dawn the next morning, July 10, the invasion force of about 150,000 Allied troops struck at different points all along the south coast of Sicily. The invasion was preceded by the landing of more than 4,000 paratroopers, soldiers who parachuted into key positions. Italians fired shells at the American ships from positions on the hillsides of Sicily. Navy ships fired back until the enemy fire ceased. Axis planes attempted to dive-bomb the invasion force but met with stiff resistance.

The sheer numbers of Allied ships and planes allowed the invasion to start fairly smoothly. Initially, the forces on the perimeter of Sicily were outnumbered and overpowered. Waves of American troops went ashore to begin the next task—working their way north to secure the entire 160-mile-long (260 km) island. Meanwhile, the beaches kept receiving more men and more equipment. Tanks and jeeps rolled ashore. Telephone wires were laid and ammunition was unloaded. The secured beaches would serve as the nerve center for the operations in Sicily.

The Axis resistance in the mountainous north of Sicily was strong. The Germans blew up hundreds of bridges, slowing down the Allied advance. Sicilian minefields laid by the waiting Germans claimed many American lives. German bombers flew over regularly and caused some damage. However, on August 17, the Sicily campaign officially ended as the town of Messina was finally taken. The U.S. Seventh Army fought beside the British Eighth Army to send the Germans fleeing across the narrow Strait of Messina into Italy. In total, 157,000 Italians and Germans were killed or captured, while another 110,000 troops escaped into Italy.

Italy

The Allied bombing of Italy on July 19 killed and injured thousands of Italian civilians. Clearly, bombing alone would not win the war. The invasion of mainland Italy was planned for late summer. Once Sicily was in Allied hands, the invasion of Italy became a possibility. Two British divisions struck from Messina on September 3, 1943, into the "toe" of the Italian "boot." Four American divisions followed from Palermo, Sicily, and Africa a few days later. The Italian government had already overthrown Mussolini, and the new leader Pietro Badoglio (1871–1957) realized the Allies were coming. On September 8, sensing that the Italian people were sick of being ruled by Germany, he also

➤ **The fighting in Sicily left many buildings in ruins.**

➤ Five American soldiers rest "somewhere in Italy" shortly after the invasion, September 1943.

knew that staying with Germany would mean sinking with Germany. After the surrender was announced, Badoglio and the royal family of Italy escaped from Rome to an Allied safe haven. The powerful German resistance in southern Italy, especially at the coastal town of Anzio, nearly caused the Americans to retreat back to the sea. Before long, the Germans occupied Rome. They imposed strict rules on the Roman citizens for what would be a harsh, nine-month-long occupation.

Meanwhile, the invasion of Italy proceeded slowly. There was a lot of ground to cover. A huge force of German soldiers concentrated on the Italian front. Much of Italy was mountainous, making things even more difficult for the invaders. The Germans on hills and mountaintops had an excellent vantage point to spot and fire upon Allied troops. In early October, the city of Naples was taken by the Allies. The port had sustained heavy damage due to Allied bombing and to German destruction of key port facilities as they retreated. The wreckage of ships, docks, and cranes was scattered throughout the waters when the Allies entered the city. It took only two weeks for American engineers to reopen the port to shipping. This allowed vital supplies to pour into the harbor. The victories at points along the Mediterranean Sea in North Africa, Sicily, and southern Italy helped slow the German attacks on Allied shipping. From 110 ships sunk in March 1943, the average went down to 27 ships sunk for each month from August 1943 to January 1944. Fewer ships sunk meant that more supplies and weapons were getting through to the Allies.

The British Eighth Army and the American Fifth Army made good progress until the late fall of 1943. By then, German Field Marshal Albrecht Kesselring (1885–1960) had a line of fortifications built across the width of Italy about 80 miles (130 km) south of Rome. Known as the "Winter Line," the defense stopped the Allies in their tracks until well after the New Year. Particularly difficult was the old stone monastery atop Monte Cassino. Here the Germans withstood several Allied attacks beginning in January, until they were finally defeated in May 1944. Success in Italy also gave the Allies the confidence to attack Greece, which the Germans had invaded in 1941.

Advances in the Pacific

A crucial victory for United States came when a Japanese radio signal was intercepted in April 1943. Because the Japanese code had been cracked, the United States was able to learn that the Admiral Isoroku Yamamoto (1884–1943), in command of the Japanese fleet, was going to be flying to Bougainville in the Solomon Islands. American planes taking off from Henderson Field on Guadalcanal intercepted and shot down the Admiral's plane on April 18. It was an important moment for the Allies because the admiral was a key figure in planning the Japanese offense and defense. It was also revenge for the United States because Yamamoto was the designer of the raid on Pearl Harbor in 1941. So secret was this mission that the admiral's death was not even announced on American radio, or the Japanese would be tipped off that their code was cracked and would change the code.

The Pacific command was divided between General Douglas MacArthur in the southwest Pacific and Admiral Chester Nimitz in the central Pacific. Nimitz (1885–1966) had the opinion that confronting the Japanese at their Pacific strongholds would be a poor strategy. Instead, he favored hopping from one small island to another, gaining ground and cutting off Japanese supply routes on the way to Japan. At the end of June 1943, Allied forces began the grueling task of inching their way closer to Japan. On June 30, the islands of Kiriwina, Woodlark, and Rendova were assaulted. New Georgia, Vella Lavella, New Britain, and Treasury Island followed soon after. On jungle-filled, mountainous New Georgia, 10,000 Japanese troops battled fiercely with the invading Americans. It took a few months until

the entire island was secured at a loss of about 2,500 Japanese troops and 1,000 American troops. The American troops fighting in the Pacific were joined by Australians and New Zealanders, whose own countries' safety was threatened by the nearby presence of the Japanese.

➤ **Right: An American GI poses next to an overturned German tank, probably in Italy. Below: U.S. Marine with a flamethrower on Tarawa Island, November 1943. Over 1,000 marines and sailors were killed and 2,000 wounded during the invasion.**

Russians Strike Back

After Stalingrad, the Red Army was able to make more progress in fighting the Germans and succeeded in winning back more ground. In February 1943, an attempt to take back the Ukrainian city of Khar'kov failed, and the delighted Germans planned operation "Citadel"—a plan to wipe out Russian forces around the city of Kursk, about 130 miles (210 km) south of Khar'kov. The Battle of Kursk that resulted was another decisive victory for the Soviet army and also one of the greatest tank battles in history.

Beginning in July 1943, about 2,000,000 soldiers using 7,000 tanks faced each other in a massive battle. Guns blared and explosions echoed across the expansive battlefield. On July 5 alone, more than 500 German tanks were destroyed or disabled. As the battle raged on, it continued to swing in favor of the Russians. German and Russian planes fought air battles as tanks exploded below them. Soviet anti-tank artillery unloaded its fury on the Germans. In the end, more than 500,000 Germans soldiers were lost and 3,000 German tanks destroyed. While the Russians also suffered heavy losses, they did not lose as much manpower and weaponry as the Germans.

The Soviets did not stop there. Through August and September, all along the Ukrainian front, the Red Army made progress. In late August the battlefront was by the River Donets, but just three weeks later it moved west as much as 100 miles (160 km) in spots. The position where Willy H. (see Chapter 2) had been stationed near Stalino was overtaken by the Russians during the summer of 1943.

Still, even with the Soviet victories, Stalin was anxious for the Americans to launch their invasion of France, as they had been promising. He knew that it would serve as a major distraction to the Germans, figuring that they would have to move some of their troops and tanks from Russia to France. Until then, the Red Army had to work slowly to retake ground that had been lost two years before.

The Long Journey Home

Howard S., born 1925
97th Division, 387th Infantry
For many soldiers, their military service took them all over the country and the world. Here is the story of one young man . . .

As a kid in **New York**, Howard was fascinated with airplanes. When America entered the war, Howard was only 17, but that did not stop him from trying to enlist in the army air force. He faked papers to make it look like he was 18. At the recruiting station in **Connecticut**, the sergeant took one look at him and said, "Go on home and come back when you turn 18." In

April 1943, after Howard had turned 18, he was drafted into the army, and reported to camp in *Massachusetts*. He was then was sent to basic training in mosquito-ridden, muddy *Camp Blanding, Florida*. From there he was sent on to another camp in *Little Rock, Arkansas*, for advanced training. He had not yet given up his dream of serving in the air force and took an aptitude test, but gave it no further thought.

Things were heating up in Italy, and many U.S. soldiers were being killed. The United States needed replacement GIs to fight the Germans. Howard was already ordered to the railroad station to be shipped out on the first leg of his trip to Italy, when a corporal called his name and said he had passed the air force test and was excused from Italy. Howard was happy and relieved all at once. He believes that if it was not for passing the test, he would be buried in some olive garden in Italy.

Next, he was sent to *Sheppard Field, Texas*, for a couple of months to take tests to determine whether he would be a pilot, bombardier, or navigator. He tested well for pilot. At the end of 1943, Howard was sent to get specialized education in *Cedar Falls, Iowa*. He did very well there and became a squadron commander. On April 4, 1944—"a date that will live in infamy to me"—he and his colleagues were told that all those who were in the ground forces before would be sent back. He did get to live a dream and pilot a plane once before he had to leave Iowa.

With the permission of his commanding officer, Howard and his girlfriend got married before he was

 ## Make a Ration Kit

When soldiers were in one place for a long time, the army was able to set up field kitchens to serve the men their daily food. Otherwise, they had to rely on rations—prepackaged food that was designed to stay fresh and not take up too much room. Actual ration kits contained items including powdered coffee, biscuits, corned beef, and chocolate.

In this activity the goal is to make a daily ration package for yourself that takes up as little room as possible and has just enough calories, carbohydrates, protein, and fat to keep you nourished and energized the whole day.

MATERIALS

* Prepackaged foods or foods that you can wrap up that won't spoil (cereal bars, beef jerky, candy bars, peanut butter crackers, pretzels, snack pudding, potato chips, nuts, raisins or other dried fruit, cookies, hot chocolate mix, tea bags, canned meat, instant soup mix)
* Plastic storage container or small box
* Ruler
* Scale
* Calculator (optional)

Reading the nutritional labels, select compact and lightweight foods to total about 1,800 calories, about 50 grams of fat, about 40 grams of protein, and about 250 grams of carbohydrates. Try to stay below 2,000 mg of sodium or you will be too thirsty on the battlefield. This is not as easy as it sounds. For example, you will find that including only candy bars will take you past your total for carbohydrates, fat, and calories, but will be far below your protein requirements. Including mostly nuts will bring up your protein total, but will also bring up the fat total.

Fit all your selections into the smallest container possible. Measure the three dimensions of the container in inches or centimeters (height, width, length) and multiply the numbers to find the volume of the daily ration you have created in cubic inches (or cubic centimeters). Now weigh your package.

Try this activity again until you have reduced the volume and weight of your package as much as possible, then ask your parents' permission to go an entire day eating only the rations. How do these rations compare to your normal daily foods in taste? Do you feel hungry? Is this food as satisfying as regular food?

➤ Howard S. in March 1944.

winter clothes and shipped by train to **Fort Dix**, **New Jersey**. On leave before he left, he had dinner at a friend's house in **New York**, **New York**. In two days they were on a ship headed to **France**. It took 13 days to cross the Atlantic on a ship protected against U-boats by a complement of navy destroyers.

After landing in January 1945, Howard was trained at Camp Lucky Strike in France—the camps were named after cigarette brands. At this camp soldiers learned about the Germans' capabilities. Next it was on to the battlefront in **Germany**—Aachen, Cologne, the Rhine, the Ruhr Pocket, and then **Czechoslovakia**. Howard was second gunner in a mortar platoon that fired 81 mm mortars at the enemy from a distance of more than 1,000 yards (900 m).

When the European war was over, those soldiers with amphibious training were needed to go to the Pacific, where war was still raging. Howard was sent home and arrived in **Camp Shanks**, **New York**, in early July 1945. He was given a 30-day furlough before reporting for service in the Pacific. By then his pregnant wife was living in **Easthampton, Massachusetts**, but he could not stay with her for long, because when the 30 days were up, Howard had to report to **Ft. Bragg, North Carolina**.

It was early August and the atomic bomb had been dropped. Howard's division was sent to **Ft. Lawton, Washington**, where they boarded several ships bound for Japan. After 29 days at sea, during which time Howard's child was born, they made it to **Yokahama, Japan**, after the Japanese surrender.

sent to another camp for three months. **Fort Leonard Wood, Missouri**, was a hot and dusty place, and a miserable letdown after being in school to become a pilot.

From Missouri, Howard was sent by train in July 1944 to **Camp San Luis Obispo, California**, where he had a wonderful time. They had amphibious training in the bay because things were going well in Europe and they would be needed to land on Pacific islands. Things changed around Christmas. When the Battle of the Bulge showed the fight was not over in Europe, Howard and his fellow soldiers were given

★ V-Mail

There were millions of Americans in active military service during the war. Each one had family and friends at home waiting to hear from him. The government decided that soldiers and anyone writing letters to them could send their mail for free. In June 1942 the government introduced V-Mail, a new method of letter writing. V-Mail forms had two sides: one with instructions and space for an address, and the other with space for the main part of the letter. Once a soldier's letter was written, it was sent to England, where it was microfilmed. One ton of letters could fit on 25 pounds (11 kg) of microfilm. One roll of film could contain 1,500 letters. Anything that might reveal key information about locations or timing of attacks was censored—usually crossed out in black. The microfilms were then sent to the United States and printed out, folded, and placed in envelopes with the address showing. Finally the letter was sent on its way to the addressee.

In this activity you will write your own V-Mail.

MATERIALS

✻ Sheet of paper
✻ Ballpoint pen and pencil
✻ Black marker
✻ Ruler

Using the ruler and pencil, draw a horizontal line across the top of a sheet of paper, about 2 inches (5 cm) down. Now draw an address box "To" and return address lines "From" to match the example at the right. Fill in the address of the friend or family member to whom you are writing. Use the space below the top 2 inches (5 cm) to write your letter. Pretend you are a soldier in the war and make up some adventures. Tell how life is on the battlefront, or tell about some of the places you have fought.

When you are done, give this letter to a friend to "censor." Your friend will use a black marker to cross out anything in your letter that mentions a specific place or location, or anything about your weapons or number of troops or how many enemy soldiers were captured. Once your letter has been censored, take it to a copy machine and reduce it in size so it is about 4 ¼ by 5 ½ inches (11 by 14 cm). Now give it to the person to whom it is addressed. See how easy it is for the person to read and understand what you have written.

➤ A Christmas V-Mail from 1943. "Seabees" was the nickname for the 300,000 men who served in Naval Construction Battalions.

Know Your Ranks

Wearing insignia on the uniform makes it easy for one soldier or sailor to look at another and know his rank and responsibilities instantly. Below are the army and navy insignia. The ranks below the thick black line are for commissioned officers who had special training, while the ranks above the line are for enlisted men. Noncommissioned officers were called "noncoms."

In this game you will test your memory and recognition skills.

MATERIALS
* Two sheets of white felt
* Fine-point black felt tip pen
* Scissors
* Safety pins
* A friend

Cut the felt into squares (about 3 inches or 8 cm). Study the army ranks and insignia on the chart below for about two minutes. Have your friend leave the room. Pick a rank and draw the insignia on a felt square. Put the insignia in your pocket and have your friend enter the room. It is your turn to leave now. Have your friend pick a rank and draw the insignia.

When you are both ready, pin the insignia to your shirts and reenter the room. Greet your friend by his rank, for example, "Hello, Major." You will have two guesses to get it right. Next your friend has to greet you properly. Whoever is the lower rank should stand at attention and salute the higher rank first. The higher rank should salute and say, "At ease." How did you do? Try this game again, this time with navy rates. They are not called ranks in the Navy.

ARMY (as of 1943)		NAVY (as of 1943)	
	Private		Apprentice Seaman
	Private First Class		Seaman Second Class
	Corporal/T-5		Seaman First Class
	Sergeant/T-4		Petty Officer Third Class
	Staff Sergeant/ T-3		Petty Officer Second Class
	Technical Sergeant		Petty Officer First Class
	First Sergeant/ Master Sergeant		Chief Petty Officer
	Second Lieutenant		Ensign

	First Lieutenant		Lieutenant Junior Grade
	Captain		Lieutenant
	Major		Lieutenant Commander
	Lieutenant Colonel		Commander
	Colonel		Captain
	Brigadier General— 1 Star		Commodore— 1 Star
	Major General— 2 Stars		Rear Admiral— 2 Stars
	Lieutenant General— 3 Stars		Vice Admiral— 3 Stars
	General— 4 Stars		Admiral— 4 Stars
	General of the Army— 5 Stars		Fleet Admiral— 5 Stars

In September 1945, American troops were occupying Japan. It was a strange experience for Howard, after seeing action in Europe, being sent home, and then sent out again in the opposite direction to a strange land. He made the best of his time in Japan. He was finally able to return home to his family in January 1946. He was discharged in **Los Angeles, California**, in February 1946, and has lived in California ever since.

✉ *The first Allied bombers began striking in Germany in 1940. While the first few years of bombing did not have any effect on Hitler's ambitions, it certainly affected the people who had to live through the air raids. The longer the war went on, the more civilian casualties increased and more and more military and industrial targets were destroyed. By 1943, the full wrath of Allied bombing was hitting Germany. Some of the fiercest raids were conducted on the city of Hamburg on July 27 and 28, killing about 20,000 people.*

✚

We got Anna's lengthy letter of the 6th today. Many thanks. Thank God we survived the last air raids. It could have been worse. Except for one broken window in the kitchen, all was okay. After the second big raid Albert came to visit us, and at noon Carl and then Dora also showed up. We are all alright, but every night you feel the threat and would want to stay up. Many people in Hamburg are spending the nights in the air raid shelters, but that is very stressful. If all goes well we will be in Thomasberg with Peter, from August 22 to September 6.

From Friedrich, Sophie, and Anke to Anna and Albert

August 10, 1943

An End in Sight?

In December 1943, General Dwight D. Eisenhower was named as the Supreme Allied Commander for the invasion and liberation of Europe. Plans were in the works for a massive assault to end the European war once and for all, codenamed "Operation Overlord." Eisenhower had already overseen the assault on North Africa and Sicily, so he was prepared for the immense challenges of the invasion of Europe.

At a conference in Teheran, Iran, earlier that month, President Roosevelt, Winston Churchill, and Joseph Stalin, known as the "Big Three," discussed the planned invasion and other war-related topics, such as cooperation among Allied nations after the war ended. They called for Germany to make an unconditional surrender or face being completely destroyed. The Allied statement from the four-day conference said "our attack will be relentless and increasing." Also in December, General Henry "Hap" Arnold, Commander of the United States Army Air Force (USAAF), revealed that the 2,000,000-man-strong USAAF had destroyed 13,500 enemy planes since Pearl Harbor. "The enemy is reeling from unceasing pressure," he said. "Target after target is being demolished."

At the end of December 1943, President Roosevelt issued a proclamation calling for a National Day of Prayer to take place on January 1, 1944. He praised the "devotion and courage of our nation's sons" and was thankful for the "brilliant success on every battlefield." General Eisenhower was optimistic too, saying "we'll win the European war in 1944."

 # Mortar Game

This game will help demonstrate the difference between mortar and howitzer fire versus anti-tank and anti-aircraft fire.

MATERIALS

* Tennis ball
* Helium balloon on 20 to 25 feet (6–7.5 m) of long string, with a brick tied to the end of the rope
* An empty, open space, like a schoolyard, field, or uncrowded beach
* A friend

Set the brick down and let the balloon float so the string is taut. Now lie down on your back about 20 feet (6 m) away from the brick. Try to aim the ball at the balloon and throw it. Because it is hard to throw lying down, the ball will go pretty slowly. It will arc through the air and most likely not hit the balloon. Now stand up and aim for the balloon. Because you are able to throw straight and fast, you can most likely hit the balloon. This is the difference between a mortar and an anti-aircraft gun.

If you can find a hill, a shed, a sand dune, or some other similar obstacle, send your friend to the other side of the obstacle so you can't see him or her. Now lob the tennis ball over the obstacle to your friend. Have your friend yell back to you how far off you were and in what direction. For example, "It landed about 10 feet in front of me and to the left!" Adjust the direction and angle of your throw until you throw the ball so your friend can catch it without taking a step. You have just learned how to hit a target with a mortar. Only mortar squads have precise instruments that help them calculate angles to the exact degree.

Weapons of War

PISTOLS AND REVOLVERS

Pistols and revolvers are small firearms that can be carried easily. A revolver has a circular or revolving chamber into which six or more cartridges are loaded one by one. As the gun fires, the chamber spins to bring the next round into position. Pistols use an ammunition clip, a magazine that contains several cartridges that is snapped into the gun.

➤ Training handgun, .22 caliber.

The gun used to train soldiers was of a small diameter, or caliber, usually .22 of an inch. (The diameter of the ammunition is measured either in inches or millimeters.) A training pistol had a longer barrel to make it easier for soldiers to sight or line up their target and to improve accuracy.

A typical pistol used in combat, the Colt M1911A1, weighed 2 pounds, 7 ounces (1.1 kg) and was 8½ inches (22 cm) long. This gun used .45-inch bullets that came in a 7-round box magazine. This meant that it could fire 7 rounds before a new magazine had to be inserted from the bottom of the gun.

These small arms were useful for hand-to-hand combat, but could not shoot a long distance. Many battles were fought from hundreds or even thousands of feet away, and for that more powerful weapons were needed.

RIFLES

The rifle was the standard longer-range weapon of World War II, carried by the infantry troops of the army. The most common American rifle of the war was the M1 Garand. This gun weighed almost 10 pounds (4.5 kg), had a 24-inch-long (60 cm) barrel, and was self-loading. The Garand had an eight-round clip, so it could fire eight rounds before being reloaded. Many millions of these guns were made beginning in 1936. It fired a .30 caliber bullet for a maximum effective range of 550 yards (500 m), much farther than any handgun could shoot.

SUBMACHINE GUNS

The submachine gun was much larger than a handgun and fired more rapidly. Unlike a handgun, you could keep your finger on the trigger for continuous firing. The most common submachine gun of World War II was the Thompson (the "Tommy"). During the war, more than 1.5 million Tommy guns were manufactured. The Tommy was also made famous earlier by the gangsters who used it during the 1930s. At over 10 pounds (4.5 kg) and nearly 3 feet (90 cm) in length, it was still small enough for one man to carry. The gun shot .45 caliber bullets using magazines of 20, 30, or 50 rounds. The weapon had an accurate range of about 100 yards (90 m).

LIGHT AND HEAVY MACHINE GUNS

Still bigger than a submachine gun was a light machine gun. These guns were longer and heavier than submachine guns and had two or three legs. They were meant to be placed on the ground and fired. Some of these had cartridges contained in magazines and some were belt-fed. The rounds were on a belt, one next to the other. The belt was fed into the

➤ An M-2 machine gun in Leghorn, Italy.

gun and the remaining string of cartridges hung off to the side. As the gun fired, the ammunition belt was pulled into the gun at a rapid rate.

The next-larger weapon was the heavy machine gun. These were not meant to be carried by one person. They were set up on the ground, in a pillbox, or placed atop a vehicle. The standard Browning M2HB weighed 84 pounds (38 kg) and was more than 5 feet (1.5 m) long. This belt-fed gun could fire more than about 500 rounds of ammunition per minute. Its effective range was a truly astonishing 2,000 yards (1.8 km), more than a mile. All guns follow the laws of physics—for every action there is an equal and opposite reaction. The more powerful the gun, the stronger the reaction. The force of the explosion of ammunition out of the gun sends a shock wave that is known as the recoil. The recoil of the M2 was so strong that the gun had to be planted into the ground before it was fired so the earth could absorb the shock.

ANTI-TANK AND ANTI-AIRCRAFT GUNS

While the machine gun was important, larger weapons had an even bigger effect on the enemy. Many World War II battles were fought and won by the armored, weapon-carrying vehicles called tanks. Stopping and destroying these tanks was the aim of anti-tank guns.

The earliest anti-tank guns before 1941 were of a small caliber, 37 mm. These could fire shells through about 2 inches (5 cm) of tank armor if they were close enough. Before long, new tanks were built that were better armored and the 37 mm guns were no longer of any use. Quickly, 57 mm followed, and then 75 mm. By the end of the war, technology had improved to create 90 mm guns, which could penetrate almost 10 inches (25 cm) of steel armor at 3,000 feet (900 m).

These guns weighed 1,000 pounds (450 kg) and up. The greater the power, the heavier the gun. All of them were on wheels and had to be towed by military vehicles to the spot where they would be used. Anti-aircraft guns did not need to pierce armor. They needed to have a greater range to reach planes flying many thousands of feet above. Both types of guns fired at a rapid speed toward their moving targets, whether at a tank or an airplane.

➤ A 37 mm anti-tank gun, quickly replaced by more powerful guns.

MORTARS

An anti-tank gun was designed specifically to penetrate thick steel armor on tanks. The armies of World War II also needed other types of long-range weapons, weapons that would explode and send shrapnel and rubble flying through the air to destroy buildings and injure the enemy soldiers. One of these weapons was called a mortar.

It came in three pieces: the baseplate, legs, and tube. The mortar squad consisted of four people. The first gunner was in charge of setting up the legs after the third gunner set up the baseplate. The second gunner fastened the tube in place. Now the squad leader could use binoculars to spot enemy targets and call in the coordinates over the field telephone. The first gunner would then sight the mortar tube to fire at the proper angle. When he yelled "fire!" the second gunner dropped the shell into the tube, then ducked down immediately. When the detonator on the bottom of the shell hit a firing pin at the bottom of the tube, the launch was triggered. Once the shell flew out of the mortar tube, it was extremely sensitive and would explode upon impact with anything. Once in a rare while, a tree branch or some leaves got in the way. This was called a "tree burst," and unintended men lost their lives when the shell exploded.

The advantage of the mortar was that the tube could be aimed at a steep angle so the mortar shell could be "lobbed" over tall obstacles to the target. Unlike the anti-tank gun, the mortar fired at a lower speed, sending the shell at an arc through the air. The mortar squad could be hidden on the other side of a hill or behind the ruins of a building. Its range was also very good, accurate to about 2,500 yards (2.3 km)—more than a mile. A popular ammunition size for the World War II mortar was 81 mm.

HOWITZERS

The howitzer was basically a cross between a mortar and a gun. Like the anti-tank gun, it was heavy and

➤ Howitzers.

➤ The job of these high-speed tractors, armed with .50 caliber guns, was to tow heavy artillery into position.

needed to be towed. It came in increasingly larger calibers as the war progressed. The 75 mm howitzer was small enough that it could be loaded onto bomber planes. The 105 mm was an early World War II howitzer. The 155 mm howitzer was popular until it was replaced by the 205 mm howitzer. Like a mortar, the highly explosive shell was "lobbed" over great distances to the enemy's front lines.

D-DAY AND VICTORY IN EUROPE

5

>> **Allied leaders of England, Canada, and the United States knew that it was up to their armies to stage an invasion of France and defeat the Nazis in Western Europe. The Soviet Union would not be involved. It had its own problems trying to fend off the German troops that had forced their way deep into Russian territory. Through early 1944, Stalin continued to grow more impatient for the invasion of France. But Stalin would**

★ ★ ★ ★ ★ ★ ★ ★ ★ ★ ★

have to wait. The D-Day invasion of Normandy, France, was a long time in planning. Every detail had to be coordinated. Maps had to be checked and rechecked. Coastal defenses had to be analyzed to find their weak spots. For two years, troops and equipment had been amassing in England. In early 1944, it was finally time to set more definite invasion plans.

American General Dwight Eisenhower, the Supreme Allied Commander, and the British General Bernard Montgomery, the leader of the D-Day invasion force, picked June 5 or 6 based on low tides and the moonlight. It couldn't be a full moon, which would be too bright, or a new moon, which would be too dark. By the first week of June 1944, there were about 2,000,000 soldiers massed in Britain. They were ready to make the trip across the English Channel into enemy territory. Reconnaissance photographs were taken and maps were drawn and studied. There were five code-named landing points—Juno Beach, with Canadian soldiers; Gold and Sword Beaches, with British soldiers; and Omaha and Utah Beaches, with American soldiers.

Beginning on June 6, just after midnight, 18,000 Allied paratroopers jumped from low flying planes and parachuted into key areas. German flak filled the air, but the Germans did not suspect anything other than an ordinary bombing raid. Though lightly armed, the paratroopers were counting on the element of surprise to

help them take over German positions at bridges and other sites inland from the beaches where the ground forces would soon be landing. Some paratroopers were dropped off target and drowned in swampy waters. Others were killed by German gunfire before they could accomplish their mission. Those who survived helped prepare the way for "glider trains" to land. Large gliders carrying troops and anti-tank guns were towed in by planes under cover of darkness. When they neared their targeted landing sites, the planes released the gliders and the glider pilots took over. The paratroopers, carrying only light weapons, were depending on the arrival of these gliders to bring in the heavier guns.

The main force of the invasion hit the beaches at 6:30 A.M., but the invasion did not go exactly as planned. Because of fog, the air support that was supposed to knock out coastal defense guns was not completely on mark. Tremendous firepower unleashed upon the invading forces, especially the first wave to hit the beaches. In fact, 2,000 Allied soldiers died on Omaha Beach alone. These soldiers were sitting ducks for the Germans manning the guns many feet above the beach. They had an excellent vantage point from which to fire. Once the bulk of Allied soldiers had landed, they simply overpowered any shoreline defenders.

When a successful beachhead was established along the Normandy coast, more men and supplies could pour into France. During the remainder of June, the situation was still tense. German resistance was considerable. Backup was sent from the eastern front, as Stalin had hoped, to try to push the Allies back across the channel. Hitler was still confident that the Allies could be made to flee France. A gigantic storm surged through the region. It damaged much of the beach area and slowed the unloading of supplies. The city of Caen, which was supposed to be taken the first day of the invasion, was not captured until July 9. It was the end of July before the Allies were ready to "break out" of the coastal area near where they had landed. Much of Normandy consisted of small fields separated by rows of hedges, up to 8 feet (2.4 m) high and sometimes 6 feet (1.8 m) deep. These thick hedges made it very difficult for Allied troops to advance. The Germans set up their defenses behind the hedgerows, firing on the American and British soldiers who could not see their enemy.

The turning point came in mid-August. The Allies were able to isolate numerous divisions of Germans who had begun a counterattack in the Falaise area of northern France. The American Third Army came around the southern flank and to the rear of the Germans. The Canadian First Army came around the northern flank and to the rear. Only 15 miles (24 km) separated the two armies. The American First Army and the British Second Army applied pressure from the front

of the German attack. The Allies trapped the Germans in this Falaise "pocket" and were able to take 50,000 prisoners, even though many thousands more slipped through and escaped.

After Falaise, the victories came quickly until winter. Operation Anvil had dumped 50,000 Allied troops into southern France not far from the Italian border to liberate the South. With great celebration, Paris was liberated on August

➤ **American troops wade through the water to reach the beaches at Normandy, June 6, 1944.**

➤ A friendly crowd greets the Americans in the newly liberated town of San Felice, Italy, 1945.

24. Hitler's orders to destroy the Eiffel Tower and historic bridges and buildings by blowing up key parts of the city were ignored by the commanding officers in charge of German forces. Meanwhile, the Allies made further progress in Italy, liberating towns as they moved farther north. By the end of August, 200,000 Germans were prisoners of the Allies. In desperation, Hitler began recruiting 15- and 16-year-old boys and men up to the age of 60. He was hoping to avoid the full-scale invasion of the German homeland by the Allies.

With all the Americans now on foreign soil, the United States realized the need to educate the soldiers about French customs and also about the poverty the French faced after four years of domination by the Nazis. The United States Army Information Office issued a "Pocket Guide to France" in 1944, in which they reminded soldiers how the French people had helped America during the Revolutionary War. The book explained how much France had suffered during the occupation. "They [Nazis] stripped her bare.... France has been plundered by the Nazis to such an extent that the people are deprived of even the bare necessities of life. Don't make their plight more difficult by buying things that they so desperately need."

Intelligence

Intelligence is the secret gathering of information about the enemy's manpower, weapons, and movements. When dealing with millions of troops in worldwide locations, intelligence becomes extremely important. Intelligence personnel were specially trained to help gather and intercept information from the enemy. Intercepting enemy radio signals, messages, and cracking codes were just a few of the ways of gathering intelligence.

Army intelligence in the field during World War II consisted of units of specially trained men attached to different groups in the army. Many of these men could speak two or more languages—

including Japanese, French, Italian, German, Czech, Russian, Polish, and Hungarian.

When prisoners of war were taken, they were sent to the intelligence unit to be interrogated. As the Allies pushed through France after the D-Day invasion, intelligence became crucial. Nazis and Nazi sympathizers were everywhere, even after the leading edge of the German army had retreated. Some prisoners were readily willing to share information while others were not. There were many ways to get a prisoner to talk, depending on his personality and mood. Methods included making the prisoner feel safe, complimenting his army's bravery and strength, or making him very uncomfortable and uncertain of his future safety. Speaking to him in his own language could be used to comfort and help create a connection between prisoner and interrogator, or to intimidate and show that the interrogator knew a lot about the enemy's culture and political situation.

Members of army intelligence also had the dangerous job of going undercover, often at night. They listened to conversations of the townspeople or followed suspected enemy officers. Sometimes they had to hide quickly in stacks of hay or take cover in barns to avoid being seen. Other times, intelligence officers mixed with the civilians to try to coax them into revealing where Nazis might be hiding. In France, French civilians and resistance soldiers were cru-cial. They passed along information about the Germans that they overheard or came across in their work. Tapping into this huge resource of willing helpers was an important part of army intelligence.

Information that members of army intelligence uncovered could easily lead to hundreds or thousands of lives being saved. There were many intelligence heroes who quietly played major roles in helping the Allies win the war. In one case, Corporal William Harvay of the Second Cavalry, Third Army, was stopped in the street by a frantic Frenchman whom nobody else would listen to. "I heard you speaking French just now," he said, "and I have important information to tell you," he insisted to Corporal Harvay.

It was August 17, 1944, and there was much celebrating going on because the Americans had just liberated the city of Orleans, France. The insistent Frenchman was lost in the shuffle as Americans and French alike celebrated. Harvay listened patiently, though the story seemed a little incredible. It seemed that the Frenchman was a major in the French Forces of the Interior, the French Resistance. Because of his civilian job as a railyard master, he had information that a German Panzer division was on its way by railroad from the south of France to try to intercept the Americans and break up their advance.

Corporal Harvay took this information to his captain, who took Harvay and the Frenchman to

➤ U.S. Corporal William Harvay received the Croix de Guerre for his intelligence work.

Go on a Reconnaissance Mission

It was important to gather information about enemy resistance. As the Allies swept through France, every town held mysteries and surprises. With this activity you will go on your own reconnaissance mission with a friend. See how well you do in getting information back to headquarters in time!

Note: Get permission from an adult before doing this activity.

MATERIALS
☆ Small notebook
☆ Pen
☆ Small flashlight
☆ Two watches
☆ A friend

Set up headquarters in your home just after the sun sets. Remember to wear watches. You and your friend are members of army intelligence hiding in an old abandoned farmhouse on the outskirts of a town still held by the enemy. You will have to leave before daybreak. Your mission is to map out the next two blocks on your notepad. Mark each building with a large square. You will have less than 15 minutes to accomplish your mission because the soldier enforcing the curfew passes by the house every 16 minutes. You are looking for the enemy intelligence headquarters, where a meeting is said to be going on at that very moment.

For each floor of a building, mark a horizontal line in your square. For example, a two-story house would be a square with a line across the middle. For an attic, draw a triangle on top of the square. For a basement draw a triangle below the square. For each floor of a building where you see a light on, mark an "X" on that floor. The meeting is going on in the building with the fewest lights on.

When your 15 minutes runs out, be waiting in front of your home, even if you have not finished. At home base, have your friend flash the lights on and off twice at the end of the 15 minutes. This will be a sign it is safe to come back inside. If you don't see the signal, that means you missed your deadline and are about to be captured. The soldier has just turned the corner and he sees you. Toss your notebook somewhere near your house so your friend can find it after you are captured. Now have your friend come outside and see if he or she can retrieve the notebook.

their colonel. The colonel believed the story and radioed the news to General George Patton (1885–1945), commanding officer of the U.S. Third Army. The general also believed the information. Within a half hour the Tactical Air Force was off to find and attack the railroad tracks that, according to the Frenchman's story, were supposed to be carrying the Germans.

It was true! The air force succeeded in slowing and breaking up the advance by bombing the tracks and several bridges. Lives had been saved. The Americans and the French were both very grateful that Harvay was there to listen to the Frenchman's tale. For his efforts, Harvay was later awarded the Croix de Guerre, one of the highest French honors. The award was presented by General Charles de Gaulle (1890–1970), former French Resistance leader and later the president of France. Harvay's story proves the importance of intelligence. Sometimes lives can be saved and battles won simply by listening.

The Failed Plot

In Germany, a growing number of military leaders were against Hitler. As the war dragged on, they realized what much of the world already knew: Hitler was going to cause Germany to self-destruct. A number of them plotted to assassinate Hitler. The man to carry out the actual assassination would have to be someone with close access to the leader. On July 20, carrying a briefcase, Colonel Count Klaus Schenk von Stauffenberg (1907–1944) walked into a meeting with Hitler and his staff. Inside the briefcase was a bomb. It was set to go off in just 10 minutes. Stauffenberg placed the suitcase on the floor and shoved it under the table so it was only 6 feet (2 m) from Hitler's feet. After five minutes had passed, Stauffenberg slipped out of the room. Someone else in the conference room noticed the briefcase in his way as he stood looking at a strategic map on the table. He moved the briefcase out of his way to the far end of the table, away from Hitler. When the bomb went off at 12:42 P.M., several of the staff were killed or seriously injured. Hitler, though shaken, was alive and practically unharmed except for a few scrapes. Already planning for the new government, Stauffenberg could not believe that Hitler had survived. Twelve hours after the attack, Hitler went on the radio to announce what had happened. He declared that the "stupid" people who had plotted against him would be "destroyed without mercy." In the angry investigation that followed, thousands of suspected collaborators were arrested and executed. Field Marshal Rommel, hero of North Africa, was implicated in the plot and given the choice of suicide over execution.

Coastal Defense

In order to prevent an attack on continental Europe, the Germans had to make sure that the French and Italian coastline was adequately defended. Massive guns stationed along the coast could be very intimidating. Though this alone was not going to be enough to defeat the Allies, a good coastal defense was a key in slowing the Allied invasion of the continent.

In this game you will try to defend a section of coastline under your command. You have a limited number of guns available to deploy. It is your job to figure out the best places to put them so that you will have maximum coverage of the coast.

MATERIALS

★ Compass
★ Protractor
★ Ruler
★ Pen or pencil
★ Tracing paper or photocopy machine

Trace or copy the outline of the coast you have to defend. Use the picture on the opposite page. You have been allotted the following guns to deploy wherever you want along the coast. The railway gun must be deployed on a railroad car somewhere along the tracks shown on the map. The guns with their ranges and angles of fire are shown on the table.

See if you can place the guns so that an approaching fleet of ships has no "holes" to slip through as it nears the coast. Keep in mind that the larger the gun, the more damage it can do. Use the ruler to figure out the distance the gun will fire. Draw a single line into the sea if the gun is stationary or use the protractor and compass to draw two lines 10 or 20 degrees apart. Shade in the area of the sea that will be covered by those guns.

Type of Gun	Range	Angle of Fire
Three 6-inch guns	23,800 yards (21.8 km)	10 degrees
Four 8-inch guns	31,000 yards (28.3 km)	0 degrees (stationary)
Seven 11-inch howitzers	12,780 yards (11.7 km)	20 degrees
One 15-inch railway gun	26,200 yards (24 km)	0 degrees (stationary)

You probably read in the newspapers that General Eisenhower visited the Normandy beachhead. I saw him and, in my opinion, he looks just like the pictures and portraits I've seen of him. Sometimes pictures can be deceiving, but it wasn't so in his case. His bearing is very fine and his appearance magnetic. You find yourself drawn to him immediately.... I saw General Montgomery while (in England). He also made an impression upon me. Of course, he wore his characteristic beret.

Corporal Charles O., 29th Infantry

July 5, 1944, somewhere in France

✢

Visits from well-known generals were always a morale booster.

The Battle of the Two Ghosts

There are dozens of well-known battles of World War II, battles that made the headlines of newspapers and are always found in history books. However, these important battles were just a few in comparison to the thousands of smaller battles that took place throughout the war. The war involved millions of men on both sides. Practically every day, Allied and Axis forces engaged in battle on many separate occasions in different locations. These smaller battles were also important for the outcome of the war. This is the story of one of these small battles—the German 11th Panzer Division's attack near Luneville, France.

Ferdinand Sperl was a Captain in the Second U.S. Cavalry. The United States Cavalry originally used horses. During the Second World War the group became mechanized and used gasoline-powered tanks and jeeps. But the function of the cavalry was still the same as always: to flank the main army and strike the enemy quickly, then retreat to the larger advancing infantry.

The 11th Panzer Division was a tank division of the German army. It was one of the best organized and longest-lasting divisions the Germans had, holding together fully armed and under strong command until the very last days of the war. Known as the "Geister" or ghost division, the 11th Panzer was under the command of the highly respected General Wendt von Wietersheim.

Originally sent to the Russian front in the early part of the war, the 11th Panzer was redirected to France in the spring of 1944 to help the Germans hold back the Allied invasion that began on D-Day. On September 18, 1944, the Second Cavalry of the U.S. Army, nicknamed "Patton's Ghosts," was engaged by the 11th Panzer outside the town of Luneville, France. The Second Cavalry had just secured the town less than two days earlier. It was screening the southern flank of the XII Corps when the news came in that six German tanks had been spotted.

What the Americans did not know as they prepared to engage the tanks was that these were not just six isolated tanks. They were a part of the mighty 11th Panzer Division. The well-armed 11th Panzer was a threat to the smaller and more lightly armed Second Cavalry. The Germans, who were about to surround the Americans, seemed determined to push the Americans back and recapture lost ground in France. On the morning of the 18th, German tanks and artillery surprised the 42nd Squadron of the Cavalry and fired at their troops as they retreated along the road back to Luneville. The German attack left more than 120 American vehicles in flames in just half an hour.

As Ferdinand's jeep made it back to the town of Luneville, an 88 mm shell hit a nearby house. The explosion riddled the jeep with debris, dust, and shell fragments that punctured the tires. Ferdinand was unharmed, but it was a close call. Said Ferdinand, "All I remember is a blinding flash, a heavy jolt, and we were in a cloud of dust from collapsing masonry." The soldier sitting in the back seat of the jeep was injured. Before the battle was over, Colonel Charles Reed, the commanding officer of the Second Cavalry, was wounded and the commander of one of the two squadrons that made up the cavalry was killed. Though the 42nd Squadron lost much equipment, it was able to fight a day-long battle that allowed the 2nd Squadron to retreat and an American armored division to counterattack and repel the Panzer division.

The Ardennes Bulge

The quick progress of the Allies during autumn 1944 caused Hitler to make a final effort to gain ground in what became known as the Battle of the Bulge. American and British armies were arriving near the Belgian forest called the Ardennes. This was the same forest the Germans had successfully sneaked through in 1940 to invade Belgium and France. A misty, cloudy day helped the Germans advance without detection by Allied planes, which were unable to fly because of weather conditions. On December 16, the Fifth, Sixth, and Seventh German Armies struck, making a big dent in the American forces they easily outnumbered.

Part of the plan involved specially trained troops under the direction of Colonel Otto Skorzeny (1908–1976), the same crafty commando who had rescued Mussolini after Italy surrendered to the Allies in 1943. These English-speaking troops were dressed in American uniforms and dropped behind American lines. To fit in, they drove captured American jeeps. They caused confusion by snarling traffic and changing directional signs.

The first week of the German attack was deadly for the Americans. With thousands of Allies killed or captured, the Germans could take what they wanted from abandoned American vehicles and equipment. Heavy, blinding snow and cold temperatures made the going very slow. Keeping warm and safe was not easy for the Americans. The ground was hard and digging trenches was frustrating, finger-numbing work. For many, a change of clothes was not possible for weeks, and shaving and washing were rare treats. Eisenhower sent a message to his troops on December 22, that said in part: "He [the enemy] is fighting savagely to take back all that you have won and is using every treacherous trick to deceive and kill you. . . . He is gambling everything. . . . Let everyone hold before him a single thought—destroy the enemy on the ground, in the air, everywhere—destroy him!" A decision was made to shift the direction of the advancing Allied armies to the north and south in order to

cut off German troops and equipment. This monumental action involved more than 700,000 men trying to move undetected through the snow to get into position.

➤ A slow advance through the Belgian snow after the Battle of the Bulge, February 1945.

General George S. Patton, Jr.
Ferdinand S., born 1918

Ferdinand saw Patton in person on a couple of occasions. The first occurred when General Patton

► Dragon's teeth at the Siegfried Line, 1945.

addressed officers near Birmingham, England, long before the D-Day invasion. Captain Ferdinand S. was among the officers. Patton told the assembled men that they should fight hard for their country so that later, when their grandchildren were at their knee, the men could say they did something important in World War II.

According to Ferdinand, Old Blood and Guts, as Patton was known, was one of the best and strongest field generals the Allies had, "a soldier's soldier," whereas Eisenhower was a great diplomatic general. Ferdinand recalls that the officers and men of the German 11th Panzer Division admired Patton, just as they admired their own Field Marshal Rommel. Patton was quite a personality. Ferdinand remembers Patton's 1944 Christmas greeting card to his troops during the Battle of the Bulge practically ordered God to send good weather. It contained a prayer to "restrain these immoderate rains" and "grant us fair weather for battle."

Hitler's goal was to regain a large chunk of Belgian territory, including the cities of Brussels and Antwerp. However, Field Marshal von Runstedt was unable to do better than create a large bulge in the American lines, hence the name Battle of the Bulge. When reinforcements arrived and the weather cleared somewhat, the Americans were able to hold the German spearhead from further advances by protecting the town of Bastogne. The Allies flew 15,000 sorties against the German bulge by the end of December, hitting more than 800 tanks and 450 planes. Despite the shift in luck, victory was not at hand yet. Closing in around them as they retreated, the Allies sought to nudge the Germans farther and farther back. The Battle of the Bulge dragged on into the New Year, finally ending on January 28. The battle cost the Germans 100,000 casualties and the Americans 80,000 casualties.

Dragon's Teeth and V-2 Rockets

The 350-mile-long (560 km) Siegfried Line with its rows of concrete tank barriers called "Dragon's Teeth" did not work as well as the Germans had hoped. In February, the Allies penetrated the line. By March, 85 Allied divisions were ready to attack the Rhine River. By some miracle, the Americans secured the Luttendorf Bridge over the Rhine at Remagen before the Germans could destroy it. The Allies were able to cross the bridge, and the first Americans reached the east bank of the Rhine on March 7, 1945. General Eisenhower was elated by the news. Rather than a retreat and regroup, Hitler ordered his armies to fight. Resistance was again met in the Ruhr Pocket east of the Rhine. The

U.S. First and Ninth Armies encircled, then squeezed the forces and supplies that lay in the heavily industrial area, snuffing any last hope of German victory. A total of 325,000 prisoners were taken and thousands of tons of military supplies were destroyed.

Hitler's latest weapon was the newly developed long-range V-2 rocket. Once launched, it flew on its own fuel power and could go a distance of over 200 miles (320 km) to deliver its one-ton explosive shell to France, Belgium, Holland, and England. Though more than 3,000 were launched beginning in September 1944, the V-2 did not cause as much terror as the loud V-1s, known as "buzz bombs," that had been used against England in the previous years.

But the V-2 was a case of too little too late. Germany had too many other problems to deal with. On the eastern front, the Germans were losing ground rapidly. On January 12, 1945, the Russian Army began a whirlwind advance from Poland into German territory. Covering 200 miles (320 km) in two weeks, the Russians overran an area known as Silesia. This important territory produced much of the coal that Germany needed. Without Silesian coal, the Germans would lose a major source of power for factories, railroads, and power plants. The Russians also gained control of Romanian and Hungarian oil fields, further crippling the Nazis. The Germans were hanging on by a thread.

The Siege of Budapest

Eva A., born 1919

In December 1944, the Russian Army began to approach Budapest, the capital city of Hungary. Hitler viewed the city as an essential stronghold. The Germans were ordered to fight as hard as they could. The Russians pushed from two fronts, through the flat suburbs of Pest on the east bank of the Danube River and through the hills of Buda on the west bank. For weeks they remained only a few miles from the city. Bombs damaged many buildings around the city. Elza, who was the nanny for Eva's daughter before the war came to Hungary, was killed by a bomb while going out for milk.

Toward the end of December, Eva and her family moved in with a friend of a friend, a 25-year-old half-Jewish redhead named Maria, who lived alone in an apartment house in Buda. The Russians, within mortar distance, began shelling Budapest. All the windows in the apartment were blown out by the force of bomb blasts and air raids, but miraculously, the Christmas tree and all its glass decorations were not harmed. The apartment was unheated except for a small coal-burning stove, enough to heat only the maid's room. The breakfast, lunch, and dinner menus were the same—beans, beans, and more beans. They rationed the beans from a large sack and then cooked them by chipping away at ice in the bathtub and boiling them in the melted ice water. The Russians continued to close in. On December 25, they took 2,300

Latitude Longitude Tracking Game

Thousands of Allied ships made the perilous voyage across the Atlantic during World War II, but few records remain of those trips. Recently, the handwritten notes of a man named G. W. Bailey, Second Mate were found hidden, folded in a book titled *Bowditch's American Practical Navigator* (1938), a U.S. Navy Publication. Now that these notes, taken from February to April 1944, have been rediscovered, it is up to you to plot out the course of Bailey's ship and see where the convoy went.

MATERIALS

* Atlas or maps of the United States, the Atlantic Ocean, and Western Europe
* Pencil
* Ruler

Refer to the notes taken by Bailey. Plot each day's noontime location on the map. Note that the first number is the degree and the second number is the minutes. There are 60 minutes in a degree. A reading of 28-58 would be just about at 29 degrees, while a reading of 28-30 would be halfway between 28 and 29 degrees.

Where was the convoy when a submarine alert occurred? How far was the convoy from the western coast of Ireland, where German submarines liked to wait for Allied ships? What single day did Bailey's ship travel the greatest distance? What was the average number of miles traveled per day? To figure this out, measure the total trip distance from February 4 to March 8 and divide by the number of days it took.

February 4, 1944 (departed)
Latitude
28-58 N
Longitude
94-23 W

February 5
28-07 N
90-50 W

February 6
28-09 N
87-00 W

February 7
26-27 N
84-18 W

February 8
24-04 N
81-36 W

February 9
28-07 N
79-37 W

February 10
31-37 N
78-30 W

February 11
33-50 N
74-54 W

February 12
36-48 N
73-28 W
(Arrived)

February 20
39-54 N
73-22 W
(Departed)

February 21
39-53 N
68-48 W

February 22
41-43 N
64-53 W

February 23
42-54 N
60-21 W

February 24
43-54 N
56-55 W

February 25
44-35 N
52-47 W

February 26
45-12 N
48-29 W

February 27
44-35 N
44-32 W

February 28
44-19 N
42-12 W

February 29
44-18 N
39-05 W

March 1
44-33 N
35-28 W

March 2
44-46 N
31-39 W

March 3
47-56 N
29-08 W

March 4
50-20 N
26-25 W

March 5
52-24 N
21-42 W

March 6
54-24 N
17-35 W

March 7
55-06 N
12-00 W

March 8
55-42 N
7-45 E
(Arrived)

March 23
(Departed)

March 24
55-36 N
7-25 E
Near Rathlin Island. Convoy speed 6 knots.

March 25
55-26 N
13-28 E

March 26
54-55 N
18-52 E
At 18:50 to 19:30 submarine signals flown by escort. Depth charges dropped. Crew stood by stations.

March 27
53-33 N
13-28 E

March 28
51-57 N
29-39 E

March 29
50-20 N
35-18 E
At 23:42 aft starboard raft carried away.

March 30
48-08 N
39-27 E

March 31
46-06 N
43-02 E

April 1
44-53 N
47-25 E

April 2
43-05 N
52-20 E

April 3
42-12 N
55-19 E

April 4
41-48 N
60-28 E
05:15 *sighted two white rockets port side of convoy General alert sounded.*

April 5
40-08 N
65-14 E

April 6
39-35 N
70-17 E

April 7
(Arrived)

prisoners in Budapest, and by the end of December had the city completely surrounded.

Nights were spent in the basement of the apartment building. Then the fighting got worse. All who were left in the building knew they had to stay in the cellar day and night. Outside the tiny cellar windows, Eva could see the soldiers walking and hear the nearby gunfire. Huge 152 mm and 203 mm shells fell and damaged or destroyed many buildings. Unlucky civilians caught in the crossfire were killed. The siege of Budapest during January of 1945 saw some of the fiercest street fighting of the war. When the bombs hit, Eva crouched over her daughter to protect her. Windows shattered occasionally. There was a makeshift oven in the basement. Once Eva's mother made a loaf of bread, but Eva found pieces of glass in the bread as she was about to eat it.

The space in the basement was tight. Eva remembers each person was allowed only 50 centimeters across (about 20 inches) to lie down in. During this time, Eva had strep throat and for two days a high fever. As the Germans retreated from Pest on January 18 they blew up the historic bridges across the Danube. The desperate Germans were growing weaker. Rations for the soldiers were almost nonexistent. They drank melted snow and ate horsemeat. Eva also had little food. Though she was hungry, Eva refused to touch horsemeat. The very thought of it made her sick.

The situation outside was becoming more and more desperate. Unfortunately, in early February, the last pockets of heavy fighting were right near Eva's building. By February 11, Hitler realized the defense of Budapest was useless against the onslaught of Russian troops pouring into the city. He ordered the remaining soldiers to make a break for it. Out of the 30,000 Axis soldiers who tried to escape, fewer than 1,000 made it back to the safety of German lines many miles away.

When the fighting was finally over in mid-February, Russian soldiers looted many homes and raped young women. Eva pulled the bed in the maid's room away from the wall and crawled into the tight space. Any Russians who entered would not see her. She hid there for 30 minutes until finally, Maria made friends with a kind Russian officer outside, who offered to protect the people of the building from marauding soldiers.

When it was safe to go outside, Eva saw a group of about 20 German soldiers who had been captured. She remembers their torn uniforms and their sad faces. Eva waved to a Russian transport truck. They let her climb in and ride to the Gellert Hotel. There she saw a Nazi who had been hanged. She also saw a bloated body floating in the Danube. Eva found a family friend who told her of a man who was rowing people across the Danube for money. She made her way across the river by boat, walking the two miles back home all the way up Andrassy Street. She saw burned and bombed out buildings and the bodies of two Hungarian Nazi leaders hanging from a tree.

➤ Agnes (left) and her mother Eva (right) with the nanny Elza, who was killed by a bomb while going out for milk.

The Rescue of the White Stallions

As the war in Europe drew to a close, the Allies pushed deeper into Germany. On April 26, 1945, the Second Cavalry negotiated a surrender with a German Intelligence unit camped in a Bavarian hunting lodge. After the surrender, over friendly discussions, it came out that the Germans had a stash of world-famous show horses and about 300 Allied prisoners about 10 miles (16 km) away, in Hostau, Czechoslovakia.

There was one problem: the town was located in the zone to be occupied by the Russian Army. Colonel Charles Reed (1900–1979), the commanding officer of the Second Cavalry, was a horse enthusiast. Reed contacted General Patton immediately. Patton agreed that Reed should attempt to get the animals safely back into the Allied zone.

On arriving in Hostau, the small cavalry task force found more than 800 horses, including 100 Arabians, several hundred Cossack horses, and about 200 to 300 of the famous white Lippizaner show horses. There was some fighting with elements of an SS division on the Czech border, but the special rescue task force reached Hostau safely. The town surrendered immediately, as had been arranged, and the American flag was raised. The SS troops mounted a counterattack on the Second Cavalry. With help from the newly liberated and armed Allied prisoners, the attack was easily repelled. Patton and Eisenhower were able to get the Russians' liaison officer to temporarily move the occupation border line for 10 days without specifying the exact nature of their mission. The horses could now be transported into safety. The animals were a bit nervous due to the close presence of tanks, jeeps, and the sound of occasional gunfire, but only eight horses were

➤ Colonel Charles Reed (center) and one of the rescued show horses.

lost along the way. In 1963, Disney made this story into a movie called *The Miracle of the White Stallions*.

Russian Occupation
Eva A., born 1919

In February 1945, Eva went back to the apartment where her family had lived before the siege. She found that Russian soldiers were living there. Because the officer in charge thought her 6-year-old daughter Agnes was very cute, he gave Eva back all of Agnes' expensive children's furniture. The officer smiled at Agnes and gave her a thick slice of bread with crystallized sugar sprinkled over the top—a very big treat in a city that had almost no food supply. Eva did not even think of asking for her own beautiful, expensive wood furniture. She knew it was off limits, as was the apartment itself. Luckily, during the war, Eva had managed to hide some of her paintings and photo albums with relatives whose homes were not taken.

At first, Eva did not care who had liberated her city, Americans or Russians. She soon changed her mind. The Russian occupation was harsh and showed no sign of ending any time soon. There were severe food shortages. Eva sold her gold wedding ring just to get 4 pounds (1.8 kg) of sugar. Hungarians were expected to greet each other with a salute and the slogan: "Szabadsag!" meaning "Freedom!" The Russians forced everyone in her new building to shovel snow on the sidewalk and street. They also forced Eva to carry bricks down to the street level from the roof of her bomb-damaged building. After a while, she quietly slipped out of sight, refusing to do any more work. The occupation that began in February 1945 lasted almost 50 years.

Hidden Treasure

As Allied troops swept through Germany, they were met by many friendly people who were not disappointed that the Germans were losing. Still, there were many thousands of loyal Nazis. American soldiers were warned not to get too friendly with German civilians. The general attitude of the Allied soldier was to take caution in deciding who could be trusted. Those who were guilty of war crimes had to be caught and arrested. It soon became clear to the Allies that stolen money and valuables had been quickly hidden throughout Germany in advance of the Allied arrival.

On April 16, 1945, the 90th U.S. Infantry Division arrived in Merkers, Germany. Two military policemen were given a tip by a couple of women on the street about the location of a salt mine containing hidden German war valuables. When this was confirmed, dynamite was used to blast open a brick wall to get inside. The sight that greeted the eyes of the reconnaissance party was truly wondrous. About 100 tons of gold, 2 million U.S. dollars, 3 billion German marks, 1 million Italian lire, and invaluable Old Master oil paintings had been brought to Merkers a few weeks earlier for safe storage. Many of the paintings had been stolen from other European countries.

Only a few days later, members of Intelligence Team Number 10 attached to the Second Cavalry were in the town of Ash, having a home-cooked sausage meal. The proud owner of the establishment took the soldiers on a tour of the smokehouse, where the sausage was made and stored. Curiously, they passed by many fresh loaves of bread on shelves against the wall of the corridor leading to the smokehouse. Was he a baker and also a sausage maker? The man was quick in his reply that the bread was not for eating now. It was being kept in case of future food shortages.

There seemed to be problems with the man's response. How long could the bread possibly last before getting stale? The soldiers reported the story to their commanding officer. When another team went back later that day, one of the men grabbed a loaf off the shelf and cut it open to find precious gems baked inside. The five dozen loaves of bread contained a few hundred thousand dollars worth of jewels and stones. It turned out that the sausage maker was an SS officer who had taken the jewels as bribes from the relatives of prison camp inmates.

While some treasure stashes were discovered, others were not found. Also, soldiers from various countries took home illegal "souvenirs" such as jewelry and small paintings. These European treasures turn up even today at antique stores or auction houses. If they are well-known pieces, they may be identified as stolen masterpieces of World War II and returned to their rightful owners.

The End

On March 19, a crazed Hitler ordered the destruction of all infrastructures such as bridges and railroads. Anything that might be of value to the invading Allies was ordered destroyed. Rather than give up, Hitler would destroy his own country first. His mad plea to leave Germany a smoldering ruin went unheard by his generals, who knew defeat was inevitable. The people of Germany would suffer more if their country was ravaged. The end was at hand. The Americans were approaching from the west and the Russians from the east. In fact, the Russians were on the doorstep of Berlin.

With the flow of positive news slowing from a trickle to a drip to nothing at all, Hitler felt vulnerable, as if all of his most trusted staff were betraying him and he was the only one who still believed in the valor of never giving up. Though

Hitler celebrated with champagne upon hearing the news of President Roosevelt's death on April 12, he had the mistaken belief that this might be the miracle he was waiting for to turn the tide for Germany. As the situation grew more desperate, even his plans for escape from Berlin evaporated. By April 26, Berlin was completely encircled by the Russians. On April 28 the Americans met the Russians on the bank of the Elbe River. The meeting was a symbolic linking of the two approaching armies and a clear signal that the end for Germany would come in just days. On April 29, the former Italian dictator Mussolini was caught in northern Italy and executed. On April 30, Hitler and his longtime friend Eva Braun were married, and then killed themselves in his bunker, leaving orders for their bodies to be burned immediately.

The End in Germany

Helga S., born 1929

"By Christmas 1944, the Russians were approaching, the school packed up, and we took the train back home with the teachers. My brother's school could not get a train reservation and it took his teachers a long time to get the children home (early 1945). He was 13 by then. However, during our visits back home, we saw a lot of changes. [There were] constant bombings . . . fire damage, and my parents had taken in quite a few of our relatives whose homes had burned down or been destroyed. The dining room had become a bedroom, and the basement was full of beds, and then in early 1945 my father was drafted and sent to shoot down airplanes.

"Many mouths to feed and you could not find much in the stores, even with your coupons. So we took our bicycles and rode into the surrounding country, where for instance a nice platter was exchanged for a few eggs. There was no school. Most of the neighborhood children were back. There was no safe place anymore . . . and most of the time we'd rather stay home than go to the bunker. Soldiers had dug a trench in the yard between our house and the neighbor's, but since there were cutoffs in electricity, we really did not know what was going on. But our neighbor had heard on the BBC [British radio] Roosevelt had died.

"We could hear the planes, the rumble of military vehicles, guns. By now there were very few men left and the women were in the shelter, so we kids stayed together. After the 'all clear' we did like our fathers had done, we went through the house and checked for blown-out windows, and on one of those excursions my brother saw a slender fire bomb sizzling in the attic, grabbed it, and threw it out through the hole in the roof. A few days later he was looking through that hole for advancing tanks we could hear in the distance. Just then a British military vehicle came down our street. The soldiers jumped out and ran into the house and brought down my brother—they thought he was a [sniper]."

➤ German ration coupons for butter, milk, coffee, and pork, valid from February 5 to March 4, 1945.

The Allies Enter Germany

Peter W., born 1938

Peter grew up in the town of Celle on the River Aller in northern Germany. During the war, supplies were short just as they were in the United States. Food was rationed and people had to redeem little stamps to get rationed goods. Peter could see the evening sky light up when the Americans bombed the city of Hanover, 20 miles (32 km) away. Though he was supposed to stay in the basement when the air raid warnings went off, sometimes he sneaked outside. Toward the end of the war, the Germans were getting desperate because they were running out of supplies. A soldier searched Peter's house and found a bicycle belonging to the housekeeper. "I'm taking this," he told the housekeeper, who protested angrily, but the soldier took it anyway.

At the very end of the war, when the American troops reached Celle, the Germans tried to blow up the bridge over the River Aller to delay the Americans. Before they were able to do it, the Americans had secured the bridge. As the Americans marched into town, Peter watched from the window inside, but his daring older brother Klaus watched from a tree outside. The soldiers' guns were raised as they came down the street. Luckily they saw that Klaus was only

➤ American B-17 Flying Fortresses helped clear the way for ground troops entering Germany in 1945.

a boy and did not shoot him. While the Americans were in town, Peter and his brother would sometimes scramble quietly into unguarded tanks and steal the Spam and C rations that the Americans had stashed away inside.

After the Americans left, British troops entered Celle. They set up bases all over town. They took over many people's houses, forcing them to become homeless. Luckily, the soldiers decided that they only needed the downstairs of Peter's house, so the family could stay if everyone moved upstairs. The British soldiers used Peter's yard as a collection point for all weapons, boots, and military equipment that they found as they searched the town. After the war, the Allied troops kept a careful watch on the German people. During this time, whenever Peter's family wanted to drive somewhere, they had to have a special ticket in their car window showing where they were going and why. Finally, after about a year, the British soldiers left and the family could finally have their house back.

The Germans Surrender

There was not much fight left in the Germans. There was nowhere left to retreat to, no more reserves to call up, and no more new tanks rolling off the production lines. On May 2, the German army in Italy officially surrendered to the Allies. The next day the Germans in Holland and Denmark also surrendered. Elsewhere in Germany and Czechoslovakia, fighting continued for some divisions while others surrendered. With each surrender, the promise of Allied victory came closer to fulfillment.

At 1:41 P.M. on May 7, Grand Admiral Doenitz, successor to Hitler, announced Germany's unconditional surrender. A cease-fire and

➤ **German self-propelled gun of the 11th Panzer Division comes in for surrender, May 1945.**

➤ **Czechs force accused collaborators to run around in a circle while being whipped.**

the border into Germany. Angry Czech resistance fighters whipped Czechs who were accused Nazi collaborators. To many, collaborators were worse than Nazis because they were seen as cowards and traitors.

Captain Ferdinand Sperl of the Second Cavalry served on an intelligence team in charge of demobilizing 16,000 German Panzer troops who had been brought to the town of Koetzing, Germany. The fully armed German tank division surrendered to the authority of a cavalry unit of much smaller size and lesser strength. Captain Sperl was given a set of four 4- to 5-inch-thick books that listed names and sometimes descriptions of wanted war criminals. It took several weeks to search among the soldiers for wanted war criminals, get all the forms filled out, and discharge all the soldiers in the once deadly 11th Panzer "Ghost" Division. The German men also had to be checked by doctors to make sure they had no major illnesses. Before the 11th Panzer was disbanded, von Wietersheim said goodbye to his troops and thanked the Americans for their fair treatment of his division and their acceptance of the terms of surrender. While the 11th Panzer had a reputation as a respected fighting machine, other divisions were composed of SS officers who were suspected war criminals. Many of these criminals were tried in Nuremberg, Germany, for Crimes Against Peace, War Crimes, and Crimes Against Humanity.

end of all hostilities was to occur at one minute past midnight on May 9. As part of the surrender, the Germans were to reveal the location of all their underwater minefields immediately. Submarines were ordered to surface at once, remain surfaced, jettison their ammunition, and keep on their navigation lights at night. All surface warships had to report their locations immediately. Orders were also given that no German ship be damaged or sabotaged in defiance of the Allies.

There was some confusion and violence between surrender and cease-fire. For example, Germans living in Czechoslovakia were robbed of their valuables as they were sent back across

Speaking the Language

World War II put people of many different cultures and languages together in a tense situation. When invading troops met civilians on the road, or saw a few enemy soldiers approaching, it helped to know a few key phrases of the language. English speakers met French, Germans, and Russians in the course of their travels. The United States government published booklets on French, German, and other languages and cultures. The booklets helped give invading American troops an idea of what to say and how to say it in case they came across someone who spoke a foreign language.

In this activity, you will learn phonetically how to speak some important sentences in those languages. Your friend should secretly pick a foreign language. You will be an American soldier and your friend a foreign civilian. You have been scouting ahead in a village in Europe and you come across someone making wild gestures.

Your friend should pick an appropriate phrase. You must figure out what language it is and reply in the same language. See if you can stretch the conversation to at least two phrases for each person. For French and German the parentheses contain the pronunciations. Because they have a different alphabet, the Russian phrases have been transliterated into phonetic spelling.

ENGLISH	FRENCH	GERMAN	RUSSIAN
We are American soldiers.	Nous sommes des soldats Americains. (New sum day soul-DAZ uh-may-REE-kain.)	Wir sind amerikanische Soldaten. (Veer zind ah-may-ree-KAN-eesh-eh zowl-DAT-en.)	My Amerikanskiye saldaty. (My Ah-meh-ree-KAN ski-yeh sal-DAH-tee.)
Speak slowly.	Parlez lentement. (PAR-lay len-TUH-mah.)	Sprechen Sie langsam. (SPRAY-shen zee LAHNK-zam.)	Gavaritye myedleyenyeye. (Gah-vah-REE-tye MYED-ley-en-yeh-yeh.)
Come with me.	Venez avec moi. (VUH-nay uh-VEC mwa.)	Kommen Sie. (KOMM-en zee.)	Idiomtye sa manoy. (IDEO-meet-yeh sa MNOY.)
Show your identification.	Montrez-moi votre identification. (MON-tray mwa VOH-tra ee-den-tee-fee-CAH-see-ohn.)	Zeigen Sie mir Ihr kennzeichen. (TSAI-gen zee meer eer -KENT-sai-shen.)	Prid'yavitye dokumenty. (Prid-yah-VEE-tye doh-ku-MEN-tee.)
Danger! (Watch Out!)	Danger! (Dahn-JAY!)	Gefahr! (Guh-FAR!)	Astarozhna! (Ah-sta-ROH-zna!)
Don't shoot!	Ne tirez pas! (Nuh TEE-ray pah!)	Nicht schiessen Sie. (Nikt SHEE-sen zee.)	Ne stryelyay. (Nay strye-LYA-ee!)
Stop.	Halte. (Alt.)	Halt. (Halt.)	Stoi. (Stoy.)
Surrender!	Capitulez! (Cah-PEE-too-lay!)	Kapitulaten Sie. (Ka-pee-too-LA-ten zee!)	Sdavaisya! (Sda-VAH-ee-sya!)
Help me.	Aidez moi. (Ay-DAY mwa.)	Hilfen Sie mir. (HIL-fun zee meer.)	Pomogitye mnye. (Poh-moh-GEE-tye mnye.)
I'm wounded!	Je suis blessé! (Juh swee bleh-SAY!)	Ich bin verwundet! (Ish bin fer-VUN-det!)	Ya ranyen! (Ya RAY-nyen!)
Is the road bad?	Est-ce-que la route est mauvaise? (Ess kuh la roo eh mow-VAYZ?)	Ist die Strasse schlecht? (Ist dee SHTRA-suh shlekt?)	Plahaya daroga? (Plah-HA-ya dah-ROH-gah?)

6

WHEN EVERY DAY SEEMED TO BE A YEAR LONG

>> For Jews living in Europe during World War II, the regular hardships of war were magnified. Their lives were in constant danger. In the countryside, entire Jewish communities that had flourished for hundred of years were destroyed instantly. In the cities, Jews tried their best to stay alive, but hiding was a difficult task. As one Holocaust survivor remembering life at the time put it: "Every day seemed to be a year long."

✷ ✷ ✷ ✷ ✷ ✷ ✷ ✷ ✷

➤ Germany's racist views came into the world spotlight at the 1936 Olympics. At the award ceremony for gymnastics, the German gold and bronze medalists salute Hitler while the Swiss silver medalist looks on.

The first seeds of terror were planted several years earlier when Adolf Hitler seized power over Germany in 1933. Hitler was extremely anti-Semitic, or anti-Jewish. Long before he took power, Hitler vowed to do something about all the Jews that lived in Germany. Though he was probably part-Jewish himself, Hitler's hatred and his position of power as an absolute dictator helped fuel anti-Semitism in Germany during the 1930s. Books by Jewish authors were burned, and Jews were attacked and robbed as early as the spring of 1933. In September 1935, Hitler established the Nuremberg Laws, which basically said German Jews were no longer citizens of Germany, and as such, had limited rights. Jewish business owners were pressured to sell their shops to Christians at extremely cheap prices. Many jobs now required proof of non-Jewish heritage, especially government jobs. More important military positions required a non-Jewish family tree going back 200 years.

The German capital city of Berlin was selected as the site of the 1936 Olympics in 1931, before Hitler took power. By 1936, many Jewish Americans protested for the United States to boycott the games or have them held elsewhere, but in the end they went on as scheduled. Hitler viewed the Olympics as an opportunity to put on a show for the world and also to demonstrate the superiority of the German people. German Jews were not allowed to participate in the Olympics (with one exception). The Americans sent Jewish athletes to participate in the 1936 Olympics, but two of the fastest track stars, Marty Glickman and Sam Stoller, both Jewish, were pulled from competition at the last minute by their coaches. Many people at the time thought this was an anti-Jewish gesture. Though not many Jews participated in the 1936 Olympics, Jesse Owens and 17 other African American athletes dashed Hitler's hopes of proving German superiority. They won many medals and broke world records.

After the Olympics were over the signs posting restrictions on Jews went back up on the streets of Berlin. The Nazis continued down the path of destruction, chipping away at the rights and livelihood of German Jews.

In the spring of 1938 Hitler took over neighboring Austria in what was known as the *Anschluss* (merging together). It was clear that both Germany's and Austria's Jews were in grave danger. Already, about 200,000 Jews had fled Germany. Artists, writers, and scientists were among the first to realize their lives could be at stake. In the days and weeks following the Anschluss, Nazis took over Jewish businesses in Vienna and caused widespread fear and panic. Many Viennese Jews were jailed or forced to work at demeaning jobs.

At President Roosevelt's request, a conference on the refugee question was held in the summer of 1938 at the spa town of Evian, France. Thirty-two countries sent representatives to the special conference to discuss how to rescue the 600,000 German Jews. Amazingly, each country present at the conference promised either no help at all or only very limited help. The United States said it would continue to allow 27,000 Germans and Austrians to enter each year. This quota included but not was not limited to Jews. Canada said that only experienced farm workers would be allowed into their country—very few European Jews worked on farms. Australia said it would allow 15,000 Jews to enter over the next five years. Brazil said only people who had been baptized could enter their country. France said there was no more room for refugees.

So it went at the conference, even though Hitler had made it clear that he was willing to send the Jews anywhere to get them out of Germany. At that point, nobody at the conference in beautiful Evian could have guessed that in less than seven years, 6 million Jews would be dead. Instead, most countries were concerned with the Great Depression. Allowing a flood of refugees during an unstable time would simply not go over well back home.

Jewish life in Germany became even more dangerous after a Jewish teenager shot a German embassy official in Paris, France, on November 7, 1938. The teenager was angry that his parents and other Polish Jews living in Germany had been deported back to Poland and treated very poorly. The government ordered all Jewish newspapers and magazines in Germany to shut down their operations. When the embassy official died on the afternoon of November 9, immediate retaliation was ordered across the entire country of Germany. In the early morning hours of November 10, SS and Nazi party members broke Jewish shop windows and looted the contents of the stores, burned synagogues, beat up and murdered Jews, and rounded up about 30,000 men and sent them to concentration camps—some for weeks and others for months. The infamous event became known as *Krystallnacht* (crystal night) for all the shattered glass that was a result of the Nazi vandalism. About 2,000 people died as a result of Krystallnacht.

Escape

The best time for the Jewish people of Germany and Austria to escape was before World War II officially started. During the mid-to-late 1930s, it was clear to most Jews that their possessions and their civil rights were at stake. Hitler had not yet made the final decision to try to kill the Jewish population. Almost all of the German and Austrian Jews who survived World War II escaped before 1940. With the failure of the Evian conference, it was difficult to find a place that would accept them. Some used whatever means necessary to leave Europe. According to what they told the immigration officials, one man and his wife came to New York to visit the World's Fair and never returned. About 1,000 professors who were kicked out of their jobs in Germany were accepted in the country of Turkey during the 1930s.

The Jews already living in the United States were very concerned about the safety of their relatives and friends overseas and pressed the government to do something. The Wagner-Rogers Bill went before the United States Congress in February of 1939 and again in 1940. The bill was an attempt to rescue 20,000 Jewish children from Europe by letting them emigrate to America over a two-year period of time. Unfortunately, it failed to get enough support to become a law.

In England, however, it was a different story. The British Jewish Refugee Committee managed to convince the government to accept children as refugees to live with British families until the end of the war. Their story was the subject of a recent award-winning documentary called *Into the Arms of Strangers*. The so-called *Kindertransport* (children's transport) began on December 2, 1938, and ended just before the war officially started in September 1939. About 10,000 Jewish children between the ages of 5 and 17 were sent by train from Germany to Holland, then by boat to England, and by train again until they reached their final destinations. They would spend the war years living safely in various parts of England with foster families or in orphanages. Many of these children never saw their parents or other relatives again. These 10,000 children were very lucky to leave Germany when they did, because out of the 1.6 million Jewish children in Europe before the war, only 100,000 survived at the end of the war.

Thousands of Jews living in other parts of Europe were able to escape during the war, thanks to the help of friends and strangers. In Denmark, the king helped protect the 8,000 Jews when the Nazis invaded in 1940. In 1943, when Hitler began to lose patience and moved to deport the Jews, the people of Denmark hid the Jewish citizens in various homes until they could be ferried across the sea to safety in neutral Sweden. Fewer than 500 Danish Jews were deported. They went to Terezin, where most survived thanks to relentless pressure by the Danish government.

Many thousands of Italian Jews were also saved by paying guides to help them cross the rugged border terrain into neutral Switzerland. Others were hidden by families or in Catholic churches and convents. Italy was liberated by the Allied troops almost a year earlier than other parts of Europe. For these reasons, Denmark and Italy had the highest Jewish survival rates of all the countries in Europe.

Other Victims of the Nazis

Hitler was not only against Jews. He was also against anyone whom he saw as a "social deviant," someone not like the rest of the "normal" German population, including people with opposing political views. Other minorities were persecuted, especially the Gypsies, or Romani, who came to Europe from Asia 700 years ago. Millions of Polish and other innocent Slavic civilians were killed mercilessly as the Nazis pushed through Poland and into the Soviet Union.

Because the Nazis were very concerned with the "purity" of their society, Hitler sponsored a program to murder mentally handicapped people. Known as the T-4 project, the program was halted in 1941 because of public outrage over what was happening to friends and family members. Unofficially, the killings continued anyway.

At Hitler's request, the Nazis also sterilized hundreds of thousands of people with genetic defects, so these people would not be able to have children. They examined thousands of Polish children for German-looking traits, and took many away from their families to learn German and live in Germany. The children would be punished if they spoke Polish or disobeyed.

Though Hitler targeted these mentally and physically handicapped groups for destruction, no group was so carefully scheduled for complete extermination as were the Jews. The chart on this page gives a rough estimate of the numbers of victims of Nazi murder and genocide. The Germans kept careful records of the killings at concentration and death camps. Other deaths, however, were more difficult to count, so the numbers are estimates.

The total number of victims of Hitler's racism is hard to grasp. Think about it this way. If you wrote down the name of each victim on an index card and stacked the cards one on top of the other, the pile would extend 3 miles (5 km) into the sky.

Kindertransport
Anita W., born 1923

"I was born in Vienna, Austria. I was the youngest of three children. I had a very happy childhood, until Hitler marched into Austria on March 13, 1938. . . . Everything changed . . . at Crystal Night they came into our apartment, took my father, and sent him to a concentration camp, beat up my mother, and looted our apartment. It was a very scary time. . . . I don't know how she [mother] got me on the Kindertransport, I don't know how. And I have to say that 90 percent of these children never saw their parents again. . . . Not until you have a kid do you realize the very strength it takes for a parent to send children to a strange country not knowing who was going to

Numbers of people killed due to racism, cruelty, and poor conditions	
Jews (total)	6,000,000
Jews (children 17 and under)	1,500,000
Poles (non-Jewish)	2,000,000–3,000,000
Mentally handicapped	150,000–200,000
Gypsies (Romani)	500,000+
Russians, Ukranians, other Slavs	500,000+
Russian prisoners of war	2,500,000–3,000,000
Homosexuals	Several thousand

➤ Jews were not the only victims of concentration camps. This death announcement card shows a Belgian couple accused of helping the Allies. The husband, Kamiel, died on December 8, 1944, at Gross-Rosen camp in Germany, aged 70, and the wife, Alice-Leonie, at Mauthausen, Austria, on March 12, 1945, aged 63.

take care of them. . . . I left March 13, 1939, the one-year anniversary of Hitler marching into Austria. There were flags flying all over the place, parades, and I said, well, they are giving me a send-off. I went by train from Vienna to Holland, then by boat to Harwich, England. And when we came to the border, the Nazis came into our train and said, 'Anything smuggled, if we find anything, you'll all go back again.' I remember there were little kids two years old and they cried all night, cried for their mothers. They had no idea what happened to them. And a lot of them couldn't find their identity afterward. They couldn't remember where they were from or who their parents were.

"So it was very scary for us because we didn't know who was going to take care of us. We didn't know the language. We didn't know the customs. A lot of children had guilt that if they would have stayed behind, maybe they could have helped, but of course they couldn't have. You don't realize that. I wound up outside London with an elderly lady, and I was her companion. They were supposed to send you to school until you were 18 . . . but she didn't, she just wanted me as her companion. It was very lonely for me, but I had no choice. [After the air raids started] I couldn't stay because she was evacuated and I couldn't go with her because I was considered an enemy alien . . . so I went to London. I had to be on my own, try to find a job, and make a life for myself."

Note: Both of Anita's parents survived.

Another setback for Jewish refugees occurred in 1939. In May of that year, a ship called the *St. Louis* set sail from Hamburg, Germany, with more than 900 Jews who had visas and the promise to be able to land in Cuba. Instead, the ship was turned away by Cuba after negotiations failed in early June. The ship next sailed along the eastern coast of the United States, hoping to be allowed to land. Again, the answer was no. The passengers recognized the seriousness of their situation. Several young men even attempted a mutiny. As the ship headed back toward Germany, four European countries intervened and agreed to each take in some of the *St. Louis's* refugees. Except for the 200 who wound up in Britain, less than two years later, the refugees' new countries were overrun by the Nazis and most of the "rescued" Jews were eventually sent to die in concentration camps.

Ghetto

In September 1939, SS General Reinhard Heydrich (1904–1942) had the idea of creating ghettoes to isolate Jews within cities. It was agreed that this idea would be put into use when the Germans invaded Poland and the Soviet Union. The goal was to force all the Jewish people in each city or town into a small area that would normally hold only a small fraction of the people who were crowded into it. The early ghettoes in Poland held up to 500,000 people. Many people were forced from their homes into shared quarters with other family members or strangers. Food was rationed to between a quarter and a half of the normal requirements. The ghettoes were surrounded with fences, brick walls, and barbed wire to prevent escape. Because of these horrid conditions, the ghettos were filled with disease and hunger. Eventually their inhabitants either died from the poor conditions or were taken to concentration camps. Few ghetto residents actually survived the entire war.

By 1943, in Warsaw's ghetto, the remaining residents were secretly stockpiling weapons and planning an uprising. As the Nazis came in to round up 8,000 Jews for deportation, the residents resisted. The Germans, initially repelled and shocked by the attack, came back heavily armed and set fire to ghetto buildings. Fighting continued. Finally on May 8, 1943, the Nazis reached the last cluster of resistance fighters, who committed suicide. By mid-May, the Nazis had completely destroyed all traces of the 1.6-square-mile (4.1 sq. km) Warsaw ghetto.

Minsk Ghetto, 1941

Asya D., born 1924

"The Germans came at night on the 24th of June and rounded up all officials and made them give over

census records. They used them to find all the Jews. In the next couple of days, they put up a wall around a small part of the city and moved all the Jews there. Men between 18 and 45 were put on trains and taken away. That's how I lost my father. A lot of our neighbors started looting our homes. The Germans recruited a lot of them. All city officials were shot or taken away. Their families were put in the Jewish ghetto.

"We all had to work to earn food. There was a curfew after dark and anyone found on the street was

➤ Anita (standing, left) and her family before the horrors of Krystallnacht.

⭐ Jewish Star

The Star of David, the six-pointed Jewish star, has been a symbol of the Jewish religion for thousands of years. During the years of the Nazi persecution before and during World War II, the star took on another meaning. It became a way for the SS officers and cooperating local governments across occupied Europe to keep track of the Jews and mark them for mockery, beatings, robbery, and deportation. Yellow cloth stars with the word "Jude," German for "Jew," written at the center were distributed. Orders were given that all Jews must sew the stars on their clothing. Everyone was given multiple stars to ensure that their various coats and jackets each had one. Though most complied, some refused to serve as targets. One day in mid-1944, in a European city swarming with Nazis and Nazi sympathizers, a fed-up young woman in her mid-twenties tore off her star. She threw it into the gutter as soon as she rounded the corner from her building then proceeded to the movies with a non-Jewish friend. She also refused to move into the ghetto that had been set up in her city. "It was never an option," she said. Though it was hard to fight against the Nazis, some people were able to survive because of their stubborn reluctance to being singled out.

What does it feel like to be singled out based on the religion you were born into, though you may look and act the same as others? In this activity you will wear a yellow triangle, the symbol of a make-believe religion.

MATERIALS
- ⭐ Squares of yellow felt
- ⭐ Scissors
- ⭐ Ruler
- ⭐ Black or blue fine or medium tipped marker
- ⭐ Cut-off sleeves of old T-shirts
- ⭐ Needle and thread
- ⭐ Your classmates at school

Take the ruler and with the marker draw the outline of several triangles, about 3 inches (8 cm) on a side. Carefully cut out the triangles. Write in the center of each one "I am Marked." With adult supervision, proceed to sew the squares loosely onto the old T-shirt sleeves.

Use the sleeve with the triangle on it as an armband. Half of the class should wear this armband for at least one or two hours. The half that is wearing the bands must sit on one side of the room. They may not speak to the other half. The other half is allowed to participate in the lessons and answer questions while the banded half must quietly take notes. The banded kids may not talk among themselves and may not look directly at any of the other kids. Anyone who disobeys can be called out and made to sit in the corner facing the back of the room.

After two hours, each student may rip off his or her armband and throw it to the floor, saying something about why she should be allowed to return to the regular class, such as, "I am no different than you," or, "I refuse to be singled out for persecution." When all the armband kids have rejoined the class, the other half of the class must put on the bands and go to the other side of the room.

When the second half of the class is done they can throw their armbands in the trash.

➤ Jewish star

shot on the spot. I was 17 years old. My job was to load and unload trains, clean German houses, and cook food for soldiers. Every 2 to 3 days, there would be "inspection" at night, and soldiers would come and look for contraband [food, jewels, radios, money]. All violators were shipped off to labor camps. This continued for two years. People were dying, and others were killed or shipped off to camps."

The Concentration Camps

The construction of the first concentration camp was announced less than a month after Hitler took over Germany in March 1933. Dachau, near Munich, Germany, was to be a place where Hitler sent the political prisoners and Jews, a "model camp" that was not as harsh in its treatment of its prisoners as the other camps that followed. Still, of the 225,000 people who were imprisoned there, almost 32,000 died.

Concentration camps were the method that Hitler's government created to "concentrate" certain types of people in one place, removed from the rest of society. There, they could be kept as prisoners and be made to do physical labor for Germany's benefit. Some camps, such as Mauthausen in Austria, were located at the site of rock quarries. At the time Mauthausen was classified by the Nazis as the most severe camp. Prisoners who were sent there were to be worked to death.

By 1939, there were several camps in operation, including Dachau, Sachsenhausen, Buchenwald, Lichtenberg, Flossenburg, Ravensbruck, and Mauthausen. The first inhabitants of these camps consisted heavily of political prisoners and prisoners of war. Early on, the Nazis did not know how they could enact their plans to kill all the Jews. As they invaded Poland and then the Soviet Union, they executed Jews by firing squad. More than 500,000 Russian Jews were killed between July and December 1941. The Nazis held a special conference in January 1942 to discuss the "Final Solution"— how to most effectively eliminate the Jewish population of Europe. The plan was created by SS General Reinhard Heydrich, who wanted to build numerous concentration camps and systematically round up and deport all of Europe's 10 million Jews. The new camps that were built were intended only to kill prisoners, not to keep them for long periods of time. The Nazis developed a method of killing that was more efficient than shooting. They used a poison gas called Zyklon-B, which killed almost instantly.

➤ U.S. troops found rings, watches, precious stones, eyeglasses, and gold fillings, near Buchenwald concentration camp in Germany. All of these had been taken from the prisoners who were sent to their deaths.

By 1943, camps were running in most occupied countries, including Austria, France, Latvia, Estonia, Poland, Lithuania, and Yugoslavia. By the end of May 1945, more than 65 percent of Europe's Jews had been killed by Nazis or Nazi supporters around Europe.

A Family's Escape
Claudette S., born 1910

After the Germans annexed Austria in March 1938, Jews all around Europe began to wonder if maybe they should try to migrate to North or South America. Claudette's brother was in Germany during the summer of 1938. His friends decided they were going to South America. He decided to return home to Hungary. As the situation began to deteriorate throughout Europe, Claudette's husband went to the American consulate to try to get a visa. Because he happened to have been born in Italy, he was given a visa because the quota for Italians going to America had not been met yet. Otherwise, he would have not been allowed to leave Hungary. Claudette did not want to leave right away because she had an infant son. Finally, in September 1939, she was fired from her job because she was Jewish. That was the last straw. In October, she, her husband, and the baby left for Holland, from where they would sail to the United States.

After the first night in Austria, they rode a train to the border of Holland and Germany. At the border, the Dutch authorities told them about the new rules. No refugees were allowed to go into Holland until 24 hours before their ship sailed. So there they were, Claudette and her family. They stood at the border not knowing what to do. German soldiers came over and said, "Go away. If you don't leave immediately, we will arrest you." Claudette was scared. Her husband contacted the nearest Hungarian consulate, which was in the city of Cologne, Germany. "Sorry, we close at 3 o'clock," the man told him. He explained the situation, and the consulate man agreed to keep the consulate open until they got there. Once in the Hungarian consulate, the man told them to leave their passports and look for a hotel room. The family tried several hotels. At each one they were asked, "Are you Jewish?" When they answered, "Yes," they were turned away. Finally, they found a hotel that would take them in—but only because they were from Hungary, and were not German Jews.

Finally, they were able to return to the border. The Dutch let them in because their ship was due to sail soon. Claudette was relieved and started to cry, when someone told her, "Don't cry. You came from hell, but now you are going to heaven." After a voyage of eight days, they arrived in America. As the war progressed, Claudette received a letter from the Red Cross that her brothers were missing. Only later did she find out that they had been taken away to Auschwitz and Mauthausen by the Nazis. She never saw them again.

Schindler's List

Oskar Schindler was a German factory owner out to make a profit. Originally from Czechoslovakia, he moved to Poland after the Nazis took over. He decided to run his factory using cheap Jewish labor. Though at first concerned with money, Schindler noticed the growing brutality against the Polish Jews and became alarmed at what he saw. Being a man of power and influence, he used his connections to insist on keeping the Jews he employed safe from the threat of imprisonment in concentration camps. He presented the German authorities with a list of 1,200 Jewish workers. He claimed they were essential to operating his factory. Schindler's claims were only taken seriously because his factory was making much needed equipment for the German army's war machine.

The list, from Szyja Abramoczyk (born 1917) to Jenta Zwetschenstiel (born 1908), contained the names, dates of birth, and supposed occupations of the Jews. Many of these people had no skills at all relating to factory work. Ranging in age from about 15 to 60, the people of Schindler's List were another example of how one person could make a difference and save the lives of many. A 1993 award-winning film called *Schindler's List*, directed by Steven Spielberg, first brought Oskar Schindler to the attention of the world.

Taken to Dachau

Laszlo M., born 1913

Laszlo was taken to the Dachau concentration camp by train in October 1944. Of the 200 Hungarians who were taken to the camp that day, Laszlo was one of only four who were still alive when General Patton's Third Army freed the camp on April 29, 1945.

Laszlo's grandmother, mother, and sister were also taken away in 1944 to a different camp on a freight train. His grandmother died on the crowded train. These trips to the camps could take as long as 72 hours, and many elderly people died of heart attacks from fear, heat, thirst, and lack of air. Laszlo's mother and sister were later killed in the gas chamber. Early during the war, Laszlo explained, when the world was still not aware of what went on in concentration camps, escapees told the public the truth about how thousands of people were being killed every day. Laszlo said after that, everyone knew what was going on, and yet still nobody did anything to stop the murders.

After the war, Laszlo was imprisoned by the communists for being a member of the wrong party. Both the German and Hungarian governments started sending him monthly checks to compensate him for the time he spent in Germany and Hungary performing forced labor. He was happy that he was finally getting repaid for his difficult wartime experiences. After 55 years, he felt there was finally some justice. The extra money made his life a little bit better.

"Paradise"

The Nazis were aware that the rest of the world was watching their treatment of the Jews. Even toward the end of the war, many people did not know what was really taking place at the camps, nor did they believe the rumors of the murders. The creation of the "model" camp of Terezin helped fool the world. Translated as *Theresienstadt* in German, Terezin, a small town of 7,000 in German-occupied Czechoslovakia, was converted into a camp and ghetto in 1941. The Nazis sent most of the Czechoslovakian Jews, as well as prominent authors, musicians, singers, composers, conductors, and artists to live in the so-called "paradise camp." Secretly, however, they deported most of the residents to extermination camps as the new residents were brought into Terezin. A library of many thousands of books was established. The Nazis even ordered the printing of paper money. With an engraving of Moses holding a stone tablet on the front and a Jewish star on both sides, the money looked and felt real. But it was of little use to the suffering ghetto residents. Children used it to play

➤ A 10-kronen banknote issued for the Jews of Terezin concentration camp. Designed to impress the outside world, the money had little meaning to starving, disease-ridden inhabitants. Children used it as play money.

a homemade ghetto version of the popular board game Monopoly.

More than 50,000 people were crammed into the little town, far more than its capacity. Beatings, hunger, and disease ravaged the population. But the Nazis tried hard to keep up the deception. An upcoming Red Cross visit in June 1944 led to a major clean-up effort. Flowers and shrubs were planted. Buildings were cleaned. Parks were created. The ghetto residents were ordered not to say anything bad about their lives in Terezin. Anyone who painted or drew pictures showing the real conditions in Terezin was killed. A children's opera and a well-known musical piece by Verdi were staged during the Red Cross visit. Clean-looking children played outside. The Red Cross delegation left Terezin with praise for the conditions. They did not know that the Nazis had sent 12,000 residents to be exterminated so Terezin did not look so overcrowded.

In the end, more than 30,000 residents of the Terezin ghetto either died there or were killed at an extermination camp after a short stay. Only 5 percent of those people deported from Terezin actually survived. Rescued by a friend, an opera manuscript written at Terezin by the doomed composer Viktor Ullman, was performed for the first time in 1975 to excellent reviews. As a memorial to the Terezin experience, a group was formed called the Terezin Chamber Music Foundation. Dedicated to performing at the Terezin

Ghetto Museum and around the world, the foundation plays the music of those who died in the Holocaust.

Auschwitz

The most notorious and deadly of all the camps in the Nazi system was Auschwitz. Two million people died in the huge Auschwitz-Birkenau complex. Unlike Terezin and other concentration camps, Auschwitz was an extermination camp, also known as a death camp. Most prisoners in death camps were killed almost immediately upon arrival. They were told that they had to take a shower. Instead they were sent to the gas chambers. Elaborately planned, these so-called "shower" rooms filled with deadly gas that killed those inside in less than three minutes. After death, the bodies were burned in ovens, or crematoria. Overall, almost 1,000,000 people were killed immediately upon arrival. The rest were assigned prisoner numbers. The Nazis tried hard to hide the mass killings from other inmates and from the rest of the world. When a teenaged girl miraculously survived the gassing because she was at the bottom of a pile of bodies and did not breathe in too much gas, it was decided that she should be shot and killed.

The *Sonderkommand* (special command) was a group of prisoners in charge of removing valuables from the bodies of the dead. They helped to dispose of the bodies. These prisoners were usually the stronger men in the camp, but their jobs did not guarantee them anything except certain death after a few weeks.

In January 1945, when the Russian army drew near, the camp was evacuated. But the prisoners were not freed. So fanatical were the Nazis about killing the Jews that the inmates were made to march to the next-nearest camp. About 15,000 of the 66,000 prisoners died along the route.

The Nazis who ran the concentration and extermination camps made sure they stripped the inmates of all their personal possessions, including jewelry, clothes, hats, and shoes. Even gold fillings in teeth were removed and melted into bullion. When the Russians liberated Auschwitz in 1945, they found a warehouse stocked with stolen property taken from the prisoners. There were 350,000 men's suits and 837,000 women's outfits. The Nazis also shaved the heads of the prisoners and shipped the hair back to Germany for use in making wigs. When they arrived at Auschwitz, the Russians found more than 7 tons of packed hair.

The Horrors of Gunskirchen Lager
Frigyes G., born 1924

"On May 10, 1944, I got notice to join the army—the 701/103 Assistant Civil Defense Division. We were

► Young Frigyes in happier times (1935).

stationed in a school, and our job was to clean up the debris and help save people after Allied air raids. I worked with enthusiasm, but why, I don't know. The terror of the Hungarian Nazis began. On November 27, the deportation of the work army of Budapest began. The armed Hungarian Nazis started shooting at random. They surrounded our quarter and made us form a line and led us to the Józsefváros Railway Station, where we boarded the cattle train cars, which were locked, and without food for two days. We proceeded to the border with Austria.

"Here we had to dig armored traps. A very cold wind that blew right through you was present the whole time. We were almost finished when the Russian army approached and we were driven towards the city of Wiener-Neustadt [45 miles (72 km) south of Vienna], Austria. To that point there had been no problem with food. We got food from the peasants in exchange for gold rings or money on the way. As we marched toward Wiener-Neustadt, there were atrocities; the Nazis beat those who could not keep up.

"From the suburbs of Vienna, we were taken by train to Mauthausen [90 miles (145 km) west of Vienna]. This was a huge concentration camp. Here we were treated with some provisions—soup and bread, maybe coffee. We were there for two weeks, in huge tents. But again the Russians advanced farther. It was the end of March now. We were marched to Gunskirchen, about 35 miles (55 km) away [to the west]. It took three days, and many weakened men who could not keep up the pace sat down to rest and were executed by the SS officers who marched us.

"On the first resting night of the march there was bread distribution, the second night a miracle happened and we had a little hot wine from kettles. I also stood in line twice with my food tin. Unfortunately, a great many men because of lack of strength were not willing or able to go for the food and nicely, quietly fell asleep [died].

"After we arrived at the Gunskirchen camp, we found that there were not enough barracks for 10,000 men [at its peak two weeks later there were about 17,000 to 20,000 men at Gunskirchen]. It was so crowded there, that in the best-case scenario, you could sleep sitting [many people were crushed to death every night]. With the food so minimal, there were enormous numbers of dead every day.

"Every morning we had to stand on line and they counted us with German thoroughness. We cleaned the barracks every day and took the dead behind the barracks and buried them in a ditch. I was lucky because on the third or fourth day I got assigned to the kitchen. I cut wood, washed potatoes—we did not peel them; only for the SS officers we prepared them. I succeeded to work there all the way until the camp was freed.

"On the night of May 3 and 4, the SS men fled. They did not set fire to our barracks, nor did they shoot all those who were still alive. They did not massacre the survivors, we simply woke up to complete silence—not the usual whistles or shouting. Finally, some brave soul ventured outside and in an outburst of passion called back, 'We are free! The Nazis have fled!'

"That was just what the prisoners needed to struggle to their feet, and not caring about each other, stepping over one another, there was a run on the food supplies. Many did not survive those first minutes of freedom. I with some of my companions tried to make order, but with no success."

Around 10 A.M., the first American jeep arrived. The first American soldiers to arrive were willing to talk to them but only from a 30-foot (9 m) distance. An English-speaking Hungarian man whom Frigyes knew stood on top of an American jeep and addressed his fellow Hungarians. After a few hours the food arrived. Everybody got raw meat and canned food. The ones who gobbled up the raw meat got gravely sick. From there the people were taken to a hospital to recover.

The "death marches" that occurred in the late winter and early spring of 1945 killed thousands of Jews who were too weak to take more than a few steps. Conditions at Gunskirchen were among the worst seen in the Holocaust. Opened in March 1945, it was not set up to be an actual concentration camp, only a dumping ground for weak and dying prisoners at the end of the war. There was no running water, only one bathroom for the 10,000 to 20,000 inmates, no medical facilities whatsoever, and almost no food. Disease, hunger, and suffocation were the main killers at the camp, where 3,000 people were crowded into

each small barrack. All told, 119,000 people died in the Mauthausen complex. Many thousands more died at the subcamps. Less than half of the dead were Jews.

Terror Above
Maria K., born 1937

Young Maria was hidden in a Catholic convent. One day the nuns heard that the Nazis were coming to inspect the convent. The nuns rushed the Jewish children into the auditorium and under the stage. Maria had to be very quiet because the Nazis were looking for them. As she waited in silence, terrified, she heard the footsteps of the Nazis' boots on the stage above. As they spoke just a few feet above her, she held her breath until, after what seemed like an eternity, they finally left.

Intervention in Hungary

By mid-1944 almost 90 percent of Poland's Jews had been exterminated. The same held true for Germany, Austria, Latvia, and Lithuania. More than 70 percent of the Jews of Holland and Czechoslovakia were killed, along with most of the Soviet Jews that the Germans came across as they invaded Russia. But the 800,000 Jews of

Hungary remained untouched to that point. Hungary was an ally of Germany during World War I and announced itself as an ally of Germany again when World War II broke out. However, thinking it too drastic, the government repeatedly turned down requests to implement the Final Solution in Hungary. Hitler grew furious at the thought that his Final Solution would not be complete.

On March 19, German forces were sent into the capital city of Budapest. Immediately they began to implement the same severe restrictions in effect elsewhere in Nazi-occupied territory. On March 31, 1944, no employment of non-Jews was allowed in Jewish households. Yellow-colored fabric stars were distributed for Jews to sew onto their clothing, and wear those clothes at all times outside of the house. The penalty for not following these instructions could be up to six months in jail. Hungarian Nazis were known as the Arrow Cross party. In some ways they were even worse than the German Nazis. They began a crusade to jail anyone whose star was not sewn on properly. On April 21, all of the city's 18,000 Jewish businesses were ordered closed. Germans emptied Jewish bank accounts and stole valuable paintings from businesses and homes. On April 30, all Hungarian Jewish and foreign Jewish authors were ordered not to be printed, published, or distributed. Libraries were instructed not to lend these books to anyone. On May 2

Jews were prohibited from attending public baths. Between June 17 and June 24, Budapest Jews were ordered to move their families and belongings from their homes to specially designated buildings. These 2,600 buildings were marked in front with 12-inch-wide (30 cm) yellow Jewish stars. The buildings contained 33,000 apartments and 70,000 rooms. As of June 25 Jews were not allowed to entertain guests in their homes. They were not allowed in public parks. When they traveled they had to ride in the last car of the streetcar. They were only allowed to be out of their homes between 11 A.M. and 5 P.M. Seventeen thousand Jews were rounded up and sent to Auschwitz, but Admiral Horthy ordered the deportations stopped.

While the Jews of Budapest were being harassed, the rest of Hungary's Jews were in much graver danger. Adolf Eichmann, the man Hitler placed in charge of the Hungarian Jews, was beginning a rapid deportation of all the Jews in rural Hungary. Between May and June, an incredible 437,000 Hungarians were deported. Mostly they were sent to Auschwitz, where they faced certain death. The immense numbers of transports put a strain on the Germans' ability to fight the losing battle against an advancing Russian Army. Still, they persisted. By the end of August, the Jewish population outside of the capital city was virtually wiped out. Immense pressure from the world was now on Hungary to see that the remaining Jews were spared. President Roosevelt, the Pope, and the King of Sweden all made pleas to the Hungarian government.

Meanwhile, the Jews of Budapest were hoping they would be spared. As many as 25,000 Budapest Jews went into hiding in the summer and fall of 1944. They found friends, acquaintances, and neighbors to hide them. They raced to the nearest church to get baptized as Catholics, even though according to the laws conversion would no longer be enough to save a Jew. Luckily, Budapest was a large enough city in which to hide.

On October 15, 1944, Horthy announced that he was withdrawing Hungary from the Axis and was thrown out of power by the Arrow Cross. On November 8, 1944, deportations from Budapest resumed. Over the next two months more than 75,000 Jews were assembled at a nearby brickyard and marched or shipped by train to the Austrian border. Random acts of violence continued at a frightening pace. From December to January, between 10,000 and 15,000 Budapest Jews were taken from the streets or their homes. They were shot and killed along the banks of the Danube River, their blood reddening the cold water.

On November 13 the Arrow Cross ordered that a ghetto be established. By December about 70,000 of Budapest's Jews were trapped there under horrible conditions. This Jewish ghetto was crowded and food rations were limited to 700 calories per day, about half of the normal rations in prisons at the time.

The true saviors of Budapest's Jews were a Swedish diplomat named Raoul Wallenberg and a Swiss diplomat named Carl Lutz. They both took an intense interest in the fate of Europe's Jews. Wallenberg arrived in Budapest on July 7, 1944, and set up offices immediately. He was partially funded by a newly created United States agency, the War Refugee Board. The access to money helped Wallenberg get things done. He hired a staff of 250 Jews and insisted that they be exempt from wearing Jewish stars. He got his way. Wallenberg's bright idea to save Jews was to create an official document that gave Jews "Swedish protection." If he could offer proof of the protection of neutral Sweden, how could the Nazis dispute? He received permission to print only 1,500 of these passes, though, there were 175,000 Jews in Budapest. Eventually he got permission to print another 3,000. All together, Switzerland distributed 7,000 passes, Sweden 4,500, and the Vatican 2,500. A Jewish youth organization created fake passes and distributed them, saving hundreds more.

Wallenberg used the official-looking papers to rescue Jews wherever and whenever he could. He drove his blue Packard to the brickyards in the suburbs of Budapest, where Jews were being assembled for deportation, and picked Jews out

★ In Hiding

Countless thousands of Jews were saved from certain death because kind European citizens hid them in their homes, endangering their own lives. Catholic churches and convents also hid some Jews. Some of the Jews remained in hiding for months or even years, and were never discovered. Others, such as Anne Frank and her family, were discovered and sent to concentration camps. Those who hid or helped the Jews were in danger themselves.

In this activity you will try to locate good hiding places in your home.

MATERIALS
* ⚹ A friend
* ⚹ An adult helper
* ⚹ Paper and pencil
* ⚹ Flashlight
* ⚹ Two books
* ⚹ Two favorite personal possessions
* ⚹ Two folding chairs
* ⚹ A small table or cardboard box
* ⚹ A can of food
* ⚹ A journal and a pen
* ⚹ A yardstick

Search your home for a place where you and your adult helper might be able to hide. Do you have an attic? A basement? A large walk-in closet? An extra bathroom? For each possible hiding place you find, take the following notes:

What is the size of the hiding place? Under 30 square feet (2.8 sq. m) is too small. Is there enough air circulation? Is there a window? Does the window have a curtain or blinds? Is there natural light? The adult should check the security of your hiding place choices. Can a flashlight being used in the hiding place at night be seen from outside your home? Is there electricity? Is there heat? How soundproof is the hiding place? Can anyone hear you cough in the hiding place from other parts of the house, or hear your footsteps in the hiding place from other parts of the house? Is there more than one exit from the hiding place? Two is better because it allows escape. Is there a hiding place within the hiding place? For example, is there a washer and dryer room in the basement, a walk-in closet or bathroom in a spare room, or a hidden corner of the attic that is not visible right away? When you think you have found the best hiding place in your home, set up the chairs and table or box and bring the cans of food, the books, and the flashlight.

Do not tell your friend where the two of you are going to be hiding. Only say that he or she should come looking for you after one hour has elapsed. Tell your friend to announce loudly while searching, "I must see if anyone unauthorized is hiding in this house!" Now spend an hour in the hiding place with your adult helper.

Whisper. Try to read by the light of the flashlight. Write a journal entry every 20 minutes. Explain how it feels to be so isolated. How does it feel? Imagine how it would feel to spend weeks, months, or years in the hiding place without going outside. Imagine the alternative, and you will understand that for many this was the only option available to save their lives. When you hear your friend looking for you, quickly write what you believe will be your final journal entry. What do you want to tell people, either family or friends, who might find this journal?

of the lines. Sometimes he used real passes. Sometimes he used other documents to fool the Nazis into letting their Jewish prisoners go free. By the end of December 1944, the Wallenberg and Lutz passes had saved many thousands of Jews. There were another 35,000 Jews living in protected houses of one kind or another, operated mainly by the Swedish, the Swiss, or the International Red Cross.

Wallenberg Saved My Husband

Magdalena P., born 1919

"My husband was in various labor camps between 1940 and 1944. In 1944, they started marching them [a group of engineers] toward Germany. On the Austrian border, next to the border guards, there was Wallenberg, a Swedish angel. He asked, 'Who has Swedish, Swiss, or Pope's protection letters?' Luckily, through one of the boys who went for food and clothing for families before they left, we could get my husband his Swedish protection letter. Wallenberg did not let them [people with passes] go any farther. [He] cleaned up a freight train car for all of them [100 people], gave them dinner, and got them on the move back to Budapest. He also gave my husband a recommendation letter to the housing manager of one of the safe houses of the International Ghetto. That's how he was saved by Wallenberg."

Wallenberg's brilliance was in his persistence and brave arrogance. Besides making protective passes, Wallenberg was the only person of any power who was looking out for the Jews of Budapest. He communicated with the Nazi government of Hungary and with the German in charge of Hungarian deportations, Adolf Eichmann (1906–1962). When Wallenberg did not have any passes left, he fooled the Nazis by presenting them with driver's licenses and other documents that they could not read. By acting official and sounding very serious, Wallenberg was able to save the lives of thousands of Jews. Still, while the protective passes worked well, there were no guarantees. One man was walking with a friend down the street when they were stopped. They both had Swedish passes issued on the same day. The friend's pass was rejected as a fake, and he was taken away. The other man's pass was accepted, and he was allowed to continue walking.

Strong threats were made by President Roosevelt that any Hungarian officials who helped the Nazis in their efforts to deport or mistreat the Jews would be treated severely after the war ended. Because it now seemed more likely that the Nazis were going to lose the war, Admiral Horthy stopped the deportations in July. Since deportations did not resume again until the fall of 1944, many people, mostly in Budapest, were saved from certain death.

The Red Cross published a book in 1946 listing the survivors of the Holocaust in Budapest.

➤ Jews converted to Catholicism or obtained falsified papers by the thousands, in an effort to save their lives.

In other communities in Europe, a list of survivors would be a perhaps a few pages long, at the very most 100 pages. The book of Budapest survivors was 1,346 pages long, thanks in large part to the courage of a Swede named Raoul Wallenberg. When the Russians took control of Budapest in January 1945, they saw Wallenberg as a threat and took him prisoner. He was never seen again, and most likely died somewhere in Russia in a prison cell.

Liberation

The advancing Russian army began to approach the Polish concentration camps from the east by 1944, while the American army pushed into Germany, Austria, and Czechoslovakia beginning in mid-April 1945. One by one the concentration camps were abandoned.

The desperate Nazis were unwilling to free their prisoners or let them fall into the hands of the enemy, so the severely weakened men and women inmates were forced to march on foot to other concentration camps away from the front lines. Anyone who could not walk or stopped along the way was killed. The Hungarian Jews working on fortifications along the Austrian and Hungarian border were among the last waves of prisoners forced to march. More than 200,000 prisoners, of whom 100,000 were Jews, died on the dozens of "death marches," many of which occurred in the middle of winter.

The Nazis' stubborn insistence on deporting every last Jew may have contributed to their defeat. They committed needed trains, supplies, and experienced military personnel to the deportation, imprisonment, and killing of the Jews. They killed people who could have helped hold back Russian advances.

The first major sightings of concentration camp survivors occurred in April 1945. As German forces weakened, some Jews were able to escape while being transferred from one camp to another. In one instance, seven female prisoners from Hungary weighing between 60 and 80 pounds (27 and 36 kg) each, were thrown in the local jail in the town where they had escaped. They were shown sympathy by the jailkeeper's wife, who gave them raw potatoes to eat. When the women were met by an American soldier who spoke their language, they kissed his shoes.

American troops finally reaching Germany encountered columns of prisoners being forced to march by SS guards, even as they were being completely surrounded. It was from these prisoners that the Americans learned the details of where the concentration camps were located and how poorly the inmates had been treated. This information was passed on to army headquarters. General Patton ordered the camps liberated immediately.

Even when they had already heard rumors and stories of what to expect, the American soldiers who first liberated the camps could not believe what they were seeing. The stench of filth and death met them and stayed with them hours after they left. Corpses waiting to be buried were piled up or lay in open ditches. Disease-riddled, emaciated, half-dead prisoners begged for food. Some were too weak to move. Many did not live more than a week, even with nourishment and hospital care. Of those prisoners freed at Mauthausen, 3,000 died after liberation.

Getting home was an adventure in itself. Refugees wandered through hunger-stricken towns in sometimes unfriendly places. The Soviet Union controlled Eastern Europe. Anyone wandering through the Russian zone had to be extra careful. These former prisoners, still extremely weak, spent time in hospitals and temporary camps. For many the journey home took weeks and months on foot. The journey home was painfully slow for those who wondered what had become of their homes, their families, and their friends. For example, the well-known writer and Holocaust survivor Primo Levi was liberated in Poland on January 27, 1945. After a roundabout journey he arrived home in Turin, Italy on October 19, 1945, almost nine months later.

Slowly, the camp commanders and other high-ranking SS officers in charge of killings and deportations were rounded up. Many of the people tried and convicted at the Nuremberg Trials late in 1945 were charged with crimes relating to the Holocaust.

Travels Through Austria—The Long Road Home
Frigyes G., born 1924

"After having taken part actively in the evacuation of Gunskirchen with the last few men, I arrived at Horschung, a huge military airport where the Americans collected the weary, sick, and weakened men. I with some of my colleagues who helped empty the camp were given special treatment. The food was good, and we also got new clothing. I only kept my overcoat with a big yellow star. I brought this home for a souvenir. Some of my friends could speak English, so we developed a friendship with the commanding officer.

"When after a few weeks we told him we wanted to return home, he gave us a look as if he did not understand. He said that they had received discouraging information about the Russians who were on the other side of the demarcation line. There were in the meantime different organizations that tried to convince us that first we should go to Sweden, or France, or Holland, and then when the situation improves the time will come to return home. Many accepted the invitation, but I wanted to go home so I could not persuade myself to go along. Our group diminished to

➤ Not all the concentration camps survivors recovered. Many, including Frigyes' cousin Istvan, died in the hospital during the summer of 1945.

half, we said goodbye to the Americans. We somehow got a truck that they packed for us with about 20 cans of food and blankets. We also got a certificate with several signatures and two seals that said we helped the American Army and asked any Russians we might encounter to help us on our way home. We shook hands with the Americans and departed.

"The Russian zone was about 8 miles (13 km) away. Until then we did not see even one soldier. We were traveling fast, when all of a sudden, three Russians appeared. 'Stoj!' (Stop!) they said, and we greeted them laughing. We gave our American document to the brightest-looking one. They looked at it, turned it around, and in the end one of them left with our paper. That was the last we saw of either the Russian or the paper he had taken from us. We were just sitting and waiting, waiting. It became evening. There came two Russians pulling a farm wagon. They started telling us to unpack the truck because the wagon will be ours and the truck will be theirs. In the meantime, more and more Russians surrounded us, so we started to quickly remove our things. They started pushing, saying, 'Come on, come on,' in Russian and started driving our truck down the road. A lot of our boxes and blankets were left on the truck but we were happy that they let us go farther toward home without harming us. All of this happened in the

➤ Two survivors of the just-liberated Lager-Norhausen concentration camp, April 14, 1945.

pitch-dark night. Of course we did not even know where we were going, and when it started to become light, we stopped and rested. We were freezing because all the warm blankets were left in the truck. We ate something. As the morning sun began to shine, we departed. Pulling and pushing the wagon was very exhausting.

"We started meeting up with Italians, Serbs, and Ukranians, all of whom were also dragged from their countries to work and were now heading for home. Toward evening we arrived near a clearing. There were very many people here. This could have been an old quarry. It was not sympathetic, and we did not want to enter, but when we wanted to pull the wagon further a Russian jumped in front of us on a horse and told us pretty clearly that we could not travel at night because they shoot at everybody. So we stayed. We got and ate soup from a mess tin.

"In the morning came a new surprise—we couldn't leave because a bunch of Russians closed off the exit. There were horse-mounted soldiers everywhere, shouting. About 500 or 600 people all together, we had to form a line and leave on the highway. On both sides, the Russians galloped up and down.

Close to the town of Amstetten, the road gets near the train tracks. I heard a train approaching. As the train got alongside us, it slowed down and the freight doors opened up. Everybody left the line and ran up to the train. Helping hands reached down and pulled us up. The train, of course, was still on the move. The Russians shot into the air and the train started rum-bling forward faster. We didn't have a wagon, we didn't have cans of food. . . . Where were we going? Nobody knew for sure. Most got on board in Germany, and at that time the destination was Vienna, so it must be going in that direction for sure. We stopped before Vienna, got off. Fourteen of us kept together, now I was hungry again. It was about noon when we got to the first small cottage. It was sunny, and I was wobbling. Someone held my arms to steady me. We entered into a courtyard. They let us sit on a bench, gave us boiled potatoes. There came a gentleman, a doctor, who called an ambulance and all of us were taken to the hospital. A 6-foot-tall (2 m) nun came, took off my clothes, put me in the bathtub, and started scrubbing. The brown spots were not dirt but frostbite, though I couldn't remember how to say it in German. She figured it out and stopped scrubbing. She took my weight—45 kilograms (99 pounds). She let out a cry of shock.

"I was for two weeks in the hospital in Vienna. It was good. It did not even bother me that in the next beds there were German and Austrian soldiers, among them a good amount of SS."

Note: Frigyes finally arrived home on July 5, 1945, two months after being freed, to find his immediate family still intact "by some miracle."

7

PACIFIC VICTORY

>> Though Japan and Germany were on the same side during World War II, the Pacific war with Japan was almost an entirely separate war. Much of the European and African campaigns hinged on land battles across many countries. The Pacific war hinged on sea and air battles. In Europe, the goal was to move into France and Italy and make the push toward Germany. In the Pacific, General MacArthur's goal was to work his way back

★ ★ ★ ★ ★ ★ ★ ★ ★ ★ ★

➤ The tide continued to turn in the favor of the United States during 1944. At left, American troops on Saipan in 1944, and at right, Americans inspect a charred Japanese tank on the island of Kwajalein in early 1944.

to the Philippines from the south. Admiral Nimitz's goal was to island-hop across the South Pacific from one small island to the next, until the Allies were on the doorstep of Japan itself.

From the earliest victories at Midway Island and Guadalcanal in 1942, the United States pushed farther toward their goal. The going was slow, and the Japanese fought fiercely. In Europe, there were basically two big sea-to-land invasions in Italy and France. The war in the Pacific consisted of countless invasions of islands, each occupied by thousands of Japanese troops. Each

island had its own unique challenges—hills, sand, cliffs, jungles, caves—that were difficult to overcome. But the United States had little choice. To win the war, the base of operations had to get closer to Japan. Every mile of the Pacific secured by the U.S. fleet meant Allied shipping could pass through unharmed, and American bombers would have a home base closer to their main target of Japan.

Victory in the Mariana Islands in June and July 1944 helped provide the United States with their closest home base yet. Fiercely fought battles on the main Mariana Islands of Saipan, Tinian, and Guam cost the United States thousands of lives, but the Japanese lost many more troops and gave up a major stepping stone to American victory.

Pacific Duty
Sergeant William M., born 1924

William was with the 5th Army Air Force, 13th Attack Squadron stationed in Port Moresby, New Guinea, in 1944. He was the rear gunner on a three-person crew of the Douglas A-26 *Invader*, a bomber. His plane was heavily armed with 18 forward firing .50 caliber machine guns, and 4 guns in the rear controlled by William. The forward guns could fire over 5,000 rounds in just one minute. There were 2 guns in an upper turret and 2 guns in a lower turret, controlled by remote. To get from the front to the back of the plane, you had to crawl through a narrow passageway only a couple of feet wide. The plane could also carry 4,000 pounds of bombs. His A-26 had 5 rockets that could fire from each wing. Because the plane could outrun many of its opponents, the machine guns did not have to be used often to fire at attacking enemy fighter planes. After New Guinea, William was stationed at Clark Field in Manila, the Philippines. There, he was on the crew of a plane that flew medical supplies and food to the island of Okinawa and other locations.

MacArthur Returns

The road back to the Philippines would have to be paved with victories in the Dutch East Indies, the chain of large islands that lay between the Philippines and Australia. The southeastern half of New Guinea, including Port Moresby, had been in Allied control since late 1942, giving the

➤ **American planes bomb a Japanese ship near Borneo.**

➤ A view from an American bomber over Balikpapan, Borneo, probably 1944. Balikpapan was the site of the last amphibious invasion of the Pacific war, in July 1945.

Allies a good base for bombing operations. In March and April 1944, sorties of American and Australian aircraft hit key enemy positions at Wewak, Alexishafen, Hollandia, and other points on the north side of New Guinea. These sorties were in preparation for troop landings along the northern coast. The planes flew daily, sometimes up to 200 at a time. Airstrips all over New Guinea were hit heavily to prevent Japanese planes from flying during the invasion. Other targets included docks, warehouses, gun posi-

tions, supply ships, and fuel tankers. The Allies landed at the port of Hollandia on April 22, 1944. Farther to the west, toward mainland Asia, lay the island of Borneo. American planes struck at oil refineries in Balikpapan, Borneo, in October 1944. Intense shelling and bombing of the Philippine Islands from 16-inch diameter guns of nearby battleships had helped prepare for the invasion by MacArthur and his men.

On October 22, the general returned as he had promised two and a half years earlier. With him, he brought the exiled Philippine president and government cabinet members. He was accompanied by 700 ships carrying 200,000 troops. American ships off the coast were now subject to a new tactic: *kamikaze* (suicide) bombers. Knowing that they would be killed in the process, the pilots deliberately flew their planes into carriers and battleships hoping to cause death and destruction. These fighters felt honored to die a purposeful death, but many were shot down before they could crash into American warships.

The desperate Japanese decided to try to engage the full power of the American fleet into a battle and divert their attention away from protecting the invasion forces along the coast of the Philippines. Using all available strength, the Japanese Admiral Jisaburo Ozawa (1886–1966) sent a decoy fleet to lure the American Third Fleet under Admiral William Halsey (1882–1959). This tactic left behind the slower and unarmored Seventh Fleet under Admiral Thomas Kinkaid (1888–1972). Known as the Battle of Leyte Gulf (October 23–26, 1944), this was the largest naval engagement in history. It involved 32 American aircraft carriers with 1,500 planes, 12 battleships, and 100 destroyers. The Japanese plans went awry early when U.S. submarines damaged several ships in advance of the battle. Over the course of four days, airplane bombs, torpedoes, and battleship guns raged at different locations all around the Philippine Islands, but centered around the Leyte Gulf. The result was the death knell for an already weakened Japanese Navy, which lost 4 aircraft carriers and 3 battleships.

By Christmas Day, 1944, the entire island of Leyte was in Allied hands. On January 9, 1945, MacArthur targeted the main Philippine island of Luzon, where the capital city of Manila was located. By the end of February, Japanese resistance was crushed and Manila was in Allied hands. Still, island fighting in the area of New

 ## The Physics of Dropping Bombs

War planes dropped thousands of bombs during World War II, hoping to hit enemy shipping, railways, military installations, heavy industries, and factories. Many bombs hit their mark. Some did not. Dropping a bomb from a moving plane from thousands of feet in the air was not an easy task, especially with enemy planes harassing you and anti-aircraft fire coming at you from the ground. In this game you can try this out for yourself. Because the plane is moving, the bomb cannot be dropped just as you pass over the target or it will be too far ahead of the target when it reaches the ground.

MATERIALS
* Paper or plastic cups
* Candy-coated chocolates or cereal puffs (or another similar size round item)

Put the cup right side up on the ground. Stand directly over it and, holding your hand at eye level, drop a chocolate. Did you get it in the cup? Keep trying until you do. Now start from a few yards away and walk slowly in the direction of the cup. Drop your bomb just as you reach the cup, but keep walking the whole time. The candy should land a few inches past the cup. Try again. This time, release the candy before you pass the cup. Keep trying until you hit the target.

Finally, try the same thing running past the cup. You will notice that the faster you go, the earlier you have to drop the bomb to hit your target. Now imagine how difficult it was for bombers to hit their marks, especially on a cloudy or very windy day!

➤ Above: "I shall return." General Douglas MacArthur fulfills his promise of two years earlier as he wades ashore on the island of Leyte, the Philippines, in October 1944. Left: General Douglas MacArthur.

Guinea and Borneo continued for months afterward. The last amphibious invasion of World War II took place at Balikpapan, Borneo, in July when Australian troops stormed ashore. The main objective of taking back the entire Philippines was finally reached that same month.

Iwo Jima

One of the bloodiest battles of the entire Pacific war took place on a tiny, treeless scrap of an island less than 700 miles (1,120 km) from Tokyo. As with many of the United States' conquests of 1944 and 1945, this island was seen as vital to winning the war. The Japanese saw the invasion coming. They evacuated all civilians from the sandy island, leaving in their place 22,000 soldiers. These troops were dug in well, mostly hidden in underground tunnels and caves around the island. Heavy bombing by the United States in late 1944 had little effect, so when the invasion took place at 6:45 A.M. on February 19, most of the island defenses were unharmed.

The marines who hit the beaches of Iwo Jima were bombarded with mortar shells, but within four days, several were able to climb Mount Surabachi and plant an American flag on the summit. The Pulitzer Prize-winning photo of the five marines and a navy corpsman setting up the flag actually shows the second flag to be planted there. The men of the famous photo were replacing a smaller, 4½-foot-long (1.3 m) flag with a more visible 8-foot-long (2.4 m) flag.

Once the beaches were secured, supplies were able to stream onto the island. Still, it took a month to win the battle for Iwo Jima. Fanatical Japanese soldiers refused to give up, vowing to kill as many Americans as possible before dying. Americans used flamethrowers to get at Japanese soldiers hidden in caves who refused to surrender. When it was all over, the Americans had lost 6,000 men killed in action and another 17,000 wounded. Of the original Japanese force, only scant hundreds were left alive to be taken prisoners of war at the end.

In 1949, John Wayne starred in a popular film about the battle called *The Sands of Iwo Jima*. This movie accurately showed the horrors of the battle, and featured appearances by the three surviving marines who had helped raise the second American flag on Mount Surabachi. The moment is also captured for eternity in a monument called the Marine War Memorial, located in Arlington, Virginia.

Okinawa

The invasion of Okinawa was the last major invasion of the war, and one of the most hard-fought victories. This 67-mile-long (108 m) volcanic island lay only 325 miles (523 km) from Japan. In preparation for the American attack, the 120,000 Japanese soldiers had dug into positions in caves all along the narrow island. American bombing of the island was countered with Japanese kamikaze planes that damaged or destroyed several U.S. ships.

On Easter Sunday, April 1, 1945, the 10th American Army and the 3rd Marine Corps landed at Okinawa. American ships fired nearly 100,000 shells and rockets on the island that day to help the 185,000 troops who took part in the invasion. On the first day, more than 10 towns and villages were captured by the Americans as they swept across the width of the island to cut

➤ **Flag raising on Iwo Jima, February 1945.**

off the Japanese forces in the north from the forces in the south.

Though the north part of the island was taken easily, the southern end proved more difficult. Rain and thunderstorms made advances toward the southern city of Shuri a muddy mess. The immense firepower of the Americans added to the isolation of the remaining Japanese troops helped finally bring the campaign to a close. By June 7, only one-thirteenth of Okinawa remained in Japanese control.

The battle for Okinawa lasted until June 22, a total of 86 days. It was one of the most costly battles of the entire war, with 12,000 U.S. troops killed and 30,000 injured. The highest-ranking U.S. officer to be killed during World War II was General Simon Buckner (1886–1945). He was fatally injured by shrapnel while visiting the front line troops on June 18, just days before the end of the battle. Also killed was the well-known war reporter Ernie Pyle. He was killed by enemy fire on a small island off the coast of Okinawa.

The Japanese suffered far greater losses than the Americans. About 100,000 Japanese soldiers and 90,000 civilians died during the fighting compared to 12,000 American troops killed. Few Japanese prisoners of war were taken because these soldiers were trained to believe it was better to die than give themselves up for capture. Two Japanese generals killed themselves on the last day of fighting rather than be captured.

Some Japanese continued fighting and isolated firefights took place in the days that followed. A few Japanese soldiers refused to surrender until the war ended on August 14.

I have been here on Okinawa for about six weeks. I was aboard the USS Lorens for 54 days. . . . Everybody was getting so excited. Things were not quite under control then so we did not know what to expect when we arrived. But we were more fortunate than the marines that went in to Okinawa several months ago. The first night at 8 o'clock P.M. we heard our first Okinawa air raid. It lasted for a little over an hour. We had no place to stay or go. We hadn't been assigned to any squadron as yet. Just a few Jap ships [planes] tried to get through but were knocked down before they got near our airfield. But one night one [plane] was up so high our guns couldn't reach him. He let one [bomb] go by guess and killed a few men on the other hill from us. When I was assigned to Squadron Service Number 14, I was put into a 16 x 16 tent that leaked so bad all I possessed got wet. The result [was] I was pretty sick for three days.

Sergeant Joseph S., Okinawa, Marine
Corps

September 2, 1945

Home Base

George S., born 1915

George enlisted in the Marine Corps in 1943. He was
sent to Camp Miramar, California, near San Diego,
for boot camp basic training. He was scheduled to
leave on a detail to the South Pacific, but the major
in charge of the camp recognized his skills and said
he needed George to stay. George worked as part
of the Marine Air Casualty Squadron. He was responsible for receiving new recruits and shipping them out
overseas. He also received men who had performed
their required service overseas and were being sent
back to the States. He kept records for the unit and
carried out the morning roll call, as well as dealing
with the complaints of the men on base.

He rose in the ranks and by 1944 he was an acting first sergeant. He started a softball team for the
squadron that played other navy and marine and
also civilian teams. His team later became champions
of the 12th Naval District in 1944 and 1945. When
George started he played second base, but after
some time he managed the team.

The night the Japanese surrendered, his team was
playing a game about 20 miles (32 km) away from

Interview a Veteran

There is no better way to understand World War
II than to talk to someone who fought or participated in it. In this activity, you will come up with
questions and interview a war veteran. Remember,
women were enlisted too, and served key non-
combat roles during the war.

MATERIALS

* ☆ Tape recorder
* ☆ Audio cassette tape
* ☆ Camera
* ☆ Pen and paper
* ☆ Telephone book

If you do not know of any friends or relatives who
served during World War II, look in the telephone
book for the nearest Veterans of Foreign Wars
(VFW) post. Call and find out when the VFW post
will have its next meeting or event. Ask if you can
attend and talk to a veteran for a few minutes. Ask
the veteran if it is OK to take a photo.

Some of the questions you should ask are:

How long did you serve?

Where did you serve?

What branch of the armed forces were you
in? (army, army air force, navy, or marines)

Did you go voluntarily or were you drafted?

Were you confident we would win the war?

What was your rank?

What other questions can you come up with?
Think of four or five more questions and write them
down. If any of your questions make the veteran
uncomfortable, skip them. When you have finished
your interview, make sure you thank the veteran.
After you get home, you can play back the tape
and write out what the person said in response to
your questions. Put the date of the interview and
the name of the person you spoke to at the top of
the paper. Now you will have a firsthand account
of World War II to someday pass down to your
children and grandchildren!

A variation of this activity is to interview anyone who was at least five years old in 1945. As
you have seen in this book, everyone who was
alive during the war has a story to tell about what
life was like then. Though not everyone thinks his
or her story is interesting, chances are that you will
find the stories fascinating! You might questions
such as: Did you do anything for the war effort in
school? Were you scared that people in your family might be sent to fight the war? Do you remember rationing?

camp. George recalls they had a very hard time getting back to Camp Miramar. There were simply too many people out celebrating on the streets of San Diego. "It was just wild that night," he remembers. The next morning everyone around the base was saying, "When are we gonna get out, when are we going home?"

George was one of the 6 percent in the Marine Corps during World War II who never went overseas. He considers himself lucky "after seeing some of these fellows come back." When he was discharged in the fall of 1945, he went back home to Berkeley, California.

Firestorm over Japan

By the spring of 1945, America was able to concentrate all her might on defeating a weakened Japan. With air bases now located closer and closer to Japan, frequent bombing runs were possible. On May 14, 500 Boeing B-29 *Superfortress* long-range bombers dropped over a million 6-pound (2.7 kg) firebombs on the city of Nagoya, Japan. The *Superfortress* was able to carry more than twice as many bombs as the Boeing B-17 *Flying Fortress*. At 99 feet (30 m) long and 141 feet (43 m) in wingspan, the *Superfortress* was truly a giant workhorse among warplanes. It was able to fly the 3,300-mile (5,300 km) round trip from bases in the Mariana Islands successfully mainly because of its huge fuel tanks. Another 500 planes attacked again three days later, on May 17, again leaving much of the city in flames.

✉ I'm in the Pacific area on one of these many islands. I can't say where (military secret).... So Dick Stoops was killed. Tough, well maybe I can help even the score for him.

Art S.,

April 13, 1945

Other cities were targeted as well. The capital city of Tokyo was hit by a wave of 550 *Superfortresses* that dropped 750,000 bombs on industrial sites. Tokyo had already been hammered before. An incendiary raid in March had killed 100,000 people. Osaka was targeted June 1, receiving 3,200 tons of bombs dropped by 600 planes. The smoke from the fires billowed up to a height of 25,000 feet (2,600 m) into the sky. The raids continued. The city of Kobe was hit with 3,000 tons of firebombs on June 6.

⭐ Military Lingo

Just as doctors or lawyers have their own "language" with many words that are unique to their professions, people in the military also use many unique words and terms to describe their equipment and daily life.

Read the excerpts from diary entries below and look at the words in boldface. Using a dictionary, encyclopedia, military books, the Internet, or the help of someone who has served in the armed forces, try to define the words.

Excerpts from the diary of George M. Dunn, Marine Private (b. 1926)

FEBRUARY 22, 1945

We can go to **chow** in our **skivvies** if we like although no one has.

FEBRUARY 27–28, 1945

I got in some extra **sack time** these two days.

MARCH 1, 1945

At chow I learned our destination is Guadalcanal where the division is going to **engage in maneuvers**. . . . By early morning we should be back at our **anchorage**.

MARCH 3, 1945

Reveille sounded today at 0300 hours. . . . Again, as yesterday, my **outfit** did not leave the ship. . . . The navy gun crews aboard ship are having frequent **drills**. **Battle stations** sound about four or five times a day.

MARCH 6, 1945

At 1200 hours 'D' Company was called to make ready to **disembark**. . . . As we approached the beach the **coxswain** kept the speed steady.

MARCH 9, 1945

I slept on **deck** last night, but not for long. I was awakened by the raindrops, finding myself in a downpour. I made a hasty retreat to a stuffy **compartment** for the rest of the night.

MARCH 15, 1945

We are on our way to meet the Japanese. Where that will be I don't know yet. None of the boys has picked up any **scuttlebutt**. The size of our **convoy** is now twenty-two ships. We are running with an **escort** of four **destroyers**.

MARCH 17, 1945

Planes **buzzed** the convoy. They were Grumman *Hellcats* from the carriers and they flew in on us very low as if simulating **strafing**.

MARCH 18–21, 1945

There has been daily **anti-aircraft** practice for the ships' gun crews and there has been rain every day. . . . I finally learned where we are going to hit. It is an island in the Ryuku Chain called Okinawa Shima. . . . Tomorrow morning, Thursday, we are going to have a **briefing**.

MARCH 22, 1945

This morning . . . we were warned about the numerous burial tombs on the island. They are made of concrete and set into the ground and are potential **pillboxes**. The farmhouses on the island have high thick hedges growing around them and these could conceal **snipers**.

Ten days after this last journal entry, George landed at Okinawa. He remained in the beach area to help unload supplies from ships and **LST**s.

President Truman's strategy was to keep the Japanese on the defensive. Concentrate all available American firepower on each attack, he told Congress, "pinning down Japanese forces where they now are . . . applying relentless pressure to the enemy . . . so he cannot rest, reorganize, or regroup."

Food Shortages in Japan
Tsuneo Y., born 1934

Tsuneo was in the sixth grade at the end of World War II. He lived in the town of Nakajo-mura in the mountains, about 250 miles (400 km) northwest of Tokyo. Though they were not affected by bombing raids that focused mainly on the larger cities along the coast, a tremendous number of people who fled the big cities came to Tsuneo's town looking for shelter. His school was crowded with extra children. The ability of already hungry families to provide for their children was hampered by the distant relatives who came to stay with them. With most of the adult men gone to fight the war, it was mainly women and children left. Those whose families were farmers were a little bit less likely to be hungry, but they still had to sell most of their food in order to make a living. Tsuneo's father was a teacher, so his family did not have much food. He remembers scavenging for food such as chestnuts and grapes on the gentle slopes of the mountain behind the family's home. The people heard honest updates on the war until the loss at the Battle of Midway. After the battle, Tsuneo says "the information was completely fabricated." Nobody was allowed to express their real feelings about the war in public. He remembers his parents worrying about their country's future.

On July 11, 1,000 carrier-based planes bombed Tokyo and other Japanese targets for eight consecutive hours. Several battleships, including the *Iowa*, *Wisconsin*, and *Missouri*, each armed with 9 massive 16-inch diameter guns, shelled the island of Hokkaido. In July alone, American guns sank more than 1,500 Japanese ships, all but destroying their naval capabilities. This defeat gave the United States virtually free rein of the Japanese coast.

The air raids continued, getting bolder each time. On August 2, 800 *Superfortresses* dropped 6,000 tons of incendiary and high-explosive bombs on five rail and industrial cities. Residents had been warned earlier to evacuate or face destruction by B-29s within 72 hours. So powerful was the bombardment that the city of Toyama was 95 percent destroyed, Nagaoka 65 percent destroyed, Mito 61 percent destroyed, and Hachioji 56 percent destroyed. Aircraft carrier based–planes helped destroy the remnants of the Japanese sea and air power. During the last month of the war alone, Admiral John McCain's planes wrecked 3,000 Japanese planes on the ground.

Eight million Japanese civilians had fled to the countryside. Factory workers abandoned their posts and production ground to a near standstill. Food was rationed down to 1,200 calories—about half the normal daily intake. Still, it did not look as if the Japanese were about to surrender. To President Truman, a difficult decision lay on the horizon. How could Japan be defeated? The bombardment of key cities was succeeding. But was there an end in sight?

General MacArthur and other military leaders planned for the land invasion of Japan, possibly in November 1945, but estimated that untold thousands of American troops would be lost. On the Japanese side, at least as many would be killed during the invasion. Truman and MacArthur both knew that Japanese resistance on Okinawa and other islands had been fierce. Many Japanese had committed suicide rather than surrender. With the forces on the relatively small island of Okinawa taking months to overpower, how long would the islands of Japan itself take to secure? Several months? A year or more? One general estimated it would take at least 500,000 American troops to invade mainland Japan. Once that fighting was over, the war might move north, into Japanese-occupied Manchuria. Defeating the Japanese could take an additional two years, the general estimated. The future was very much uncertain during the early summer of 1945.

Atomic Bomb and Surrender

During the war the United States had secretly been working on a new weapon—an atomic bomb with ultimate killing power. The bomb harnessed the formidable energy released when "splitting" an atom of a radioactive element such as Uranium-235, called nuclear fission. This

➤ A cartoon showing American-occupied Manila, the Philippines.

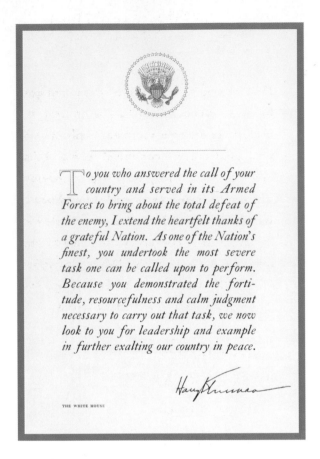

To you who answered the call of your country and served in its Armed Forces to bring about the total defeat of the enemy, I extend the heartfelt thanks of a grateful Nation. As one of the Nation's finest, you undertook the most severe task one can be called upon to perform. Because you demonstrated the fortitude, resourcefulness and calm judgment necessary to carry out that task, we now look to you for leadership and example in further exalting our country in peace.

Harry Truman

THE WHITE HOUSE

➤ **A letter of thanks sent by President Truman to troops returning home at war's end.**

energy could be used to create a huge explosion that could destroy whole cities in a few seconds and leave behind deadly radioactivity. Research on this project was conducted by scientists from all over the country, most of them working at a research facility in Los Alamos, New Mexico. Led by a scientist named Robert Oppenheimer, the project was known as the "Manhattan Project."

When President Truman received word on July 17, 1945, that the first nuclear bomb had secretly been exploded successfully in the New Mexico desert, he was pleased. Perhaps this was the only way to end the war quickly and avoid the deaths of countless American troops. What Truman did not know was that the Japanese were already preparing for an American invasion. They had begun to organize their defense plans on Kyushu, the island the Americans were planning to attack. Truman decided to use this new secret weapon on Japan. He hoped that it would intimidate them into an unconditional surrender, and that a land invasion could be avoided completely.

On August 6, a B-29 *Superfortress* named the *Enola Gay* took off from an airfield on the island of Tinian. She was flown by Colonel Paul Tibbets with a very special cargo on board—the atomic bomb. At 8:15 A.M., the bomb was dropped on the city of Hiroshima. Tibbets quickly turned the plane and flew away at top speed. By the time the bomb exploded 51 seconds later and 2,000

feet (610 m) above the city, the *Enola Gay* was 15 miles (24 km) away. The crew could easily see the telltale mushroom cloud over the city. The intense heat of the fireball nearest the detonation vaporized thousands of men, women, and children instantly. Others were killed by the force of the explosion or flying debris. About 80,000 people died within minutes that morning. Countless thousands more died later from radiation poisoning. As of midnight on August 7, the Soviet Union declared war on Japan and a few minutes later sent troops across the border into Japanese-occupied Manchuria. More than 1,000,000 Soviet troops had been assembled at the border awaiting the word to attack.

Again, on August 9, another United States B-29 dropped an even more powerful atomic bomb on Japan, this time on the city of Nagasaki, the eleventh-largest city in Japan. An additional 40,000 people were killed. The Japanese were horrified, calling these attacks "inhuman and barbaric."

Hiroshima and Nagasaki were too much for the Japanese government to bear. With Russia and the United States both fighting, things looked bleak. Would the United States continue obliterating Japanese cities indefinitely? How many lives would be lost this way? At last, on August 14, the Japanese announced their surrender and accepted General Douglas MacArthur as Allied Supreme Commander in Japan. The country would be occupied by American troops, Japanese soldiers would be immediately disarmed, and a new democratic Japanese government would be established.

On August 28, the first American occupation troops arrived in Japan. General MacArthur and more troops arrived the next day. On September 2, 1945, an 11-man Japanese delegation of officials formally signed the surrender aboard the USS *Missouri*, almost six years to the day since Hitler first invaded Poland and started World War II. Among those present were General MacArthur, an emaciated General Jonathan Wainwright, who had been a prisoner of war since the Japanese took control of the Bataan peninsula, and the British Lieutenant General Archibald Percival, who had been held captive by the Japanese since the fall of Singapore.

 At last the welcome news has come. We hope for the future that we'll never have to celebrate an event of this kind. In fact, I believe if we have another world war there'll be very few people if any left to do any celebrating. I hope the atomic bomb will be the means of making all peoples of the earth keep the peace.... There was great jubilation among our neighbors. People I haven't met before visited us, and all expressed the hope that this thing should not happen again.

Charles O. to his son, Sergeant Charles O., 69th Infantry

August 17, 1945, United States

+

The end of the war brought great joy to parents everywhere, who hoped to see their children again soon.

Victory in the Pacific
George T., born 1927

"On Aug 14, 1945, I was aboard the USS *Anthedon* in Subic Bay, just north of the Bataan peninsula in the Philippine Islands. As a submarine repair and supply ship we saw the results of war at sea even though we were not personally fighting it. Rumors had been circulating for days that the end of the war was close at hand.

"Our shipboard duties were not reduced in any way in anticipation of the war's end. In fact, the submarine USS *Bullhead* had been lost only a week before. After the workday was over, showers taken, clothes changed, and dinner consumed, we headed for preferred seating on the main deck for the evening movie. We had our mail to re-read and olive

★ Military Time

Military time is kept using a system that goes from 0 to 24 hours, with no A.M. or P.M. In the military, precision is required. Duplicate time names could cause confusion, such as 9 A.M. and 9 P.M., especially on a ship or overseas where your internal clock would be off because you are so far from home. Here is a simple trick to remember to convert military time to standard time. If the number is 1300 or greater, subtract 1200, insert a ":" before the last two digits, and insert a "P.M." after the time.

0130 = 1:30 A.M.

0800 = 8:00 A.M.

1210 = 12:10 P.M.

1305 = 1:05 P.M.

2350 = 11:50 P.M.

drab cans of peanuts to keep us busy until the movie started. Mostly, we just told sea stories and talked about home.

"Sometime during the movie, the screen went white, the lights came on, and over the ship's loud-speaker system came those long-hoped-for words: 'The Japs have surrendered, the war is over.' Pandemonium broke out. Officers and crew alike shouted, whistled, and cheered. Everything that might serve as confetti was torn up and tossed in the air. The ship's whistle was blown. Other ships anchored elsewhere also sounded whistles and shot star shells in the air. Some destroyers got underway and laid smoke screens. What a magnificent experience. I'm sure that many offered up prayers of thanks with the realization that they had survived the war.

"As one might suspect, there was a strong desire to consume some strong drink to celebrate the occasion. There was none readily available aboard ship so some drank most anything that had an alcoholic content. The favorite was an alcohol made from torpedo 'juice' [an extremely strong drink that was 160 proof or 80 percent alcohol] by some of the more enterprising members of the torpedo shop.

"I was very surprised to hear the announcement that the duty section was to report to their mustering area immediately. Naturally, I was in the duty section so my celebration was cut short. I was told that I would be standing watch on the beer locker from 2400 until 0200. I was given a Thompson submachine gun and a navy issue .45 caliber side arm,

taken to the hatch leading to the beer locker and ordered to shoot anyone who tried to break in. What an assignment! The crew members were my friends. Now, I might have to shoot them even though the war was over. I knew that I couldn't do that and literally prayed that no one would put me to the test. My prayers were answered.

"I only arrived back in the U.S.A. in December of 1945, a Pacific theater survivor not yet 19 years of age."

✉ We received news last week that the 69th was on the way home. This news we received through Mrs. Harkins who checked it with WOR [radio station] to make sure it was true. So naturally we have been very excited although there has been no news since. Gee, I hope it is true, but one can't be sure, so we better keep writing.

Natalie O., United States, to her brother Charles O., 69th Infantry Division

August 23, 1945

✝

Once the Japanese surrendered, families everywhere began to anxiously await the arrival of their loved

ones from overseas. Most soldiers did not return home right away. Some stayed on a few weeks, months, or even years more. Troops could not leave the armed forces until they received orders to return to the United States and receive a discharge. Japan and Germany were both occupied by American troops after the war. Most of them were the very same troops that had fought so hard to win the war (See Howard S. on page 78). In fact, some troops did not even ship out to the hot spots of the Pacific theater until the end of August 1945, as the war was about to end.

```
How is Dad coming on his job since the
war is over? Will it be discontinued
like 90 percent of all the jobs? It
seems like everybody is being laid off.
I guess there won't be much left for us
to do when we come home.

Sergeant Joseph S., Marine Corps, to
his mother

September 24, 1945
```

Some soldiers were doubtful there would be a place for them when they got home. Thanks to the GI Bill, help was available to veterans for education, housing, and jobs.

The generation that fought the war was very successful in life. Many got married upon their return to the United States and began families. This generation of children is known as the "baby boomers" because there was such a boom of babies born from 1946 to 1960 as veterans had children. New housing developments were built outside major cities. These suburbs featured small but comfortable houses that were very affordable for returning GIs.

Germany and Japan were occupied for some time after the end of the war. Gradually relations were normalized between the United States and these two countries. Partly as a result of the war, the State of Israel was founded as a home for the displaced survivors of the Holocaust.

The war that had cost the world 50 million lives was finally over, but even today, the politics of the world continue to be shaped by the events of the years 1939 to 1945.

★ ★ ★ ★ ★ ★ ★ ★ ★

AFTERWORD

Two hours after graduating from the Citadel Military College of South Carolina, my classmates and I received orders to report to World War II. We were young and inexperienced, but we shared a deep love of our country and the freedoms that we enjoyed. I entered combat in 1943 and fought in North Africa and in Europe as a U.S. Army officer. I understand firsthand the sacrifices made in defense of freedom. World War II was a defining moment in my life. It cultivated in me an intense reverence for my country that has guided me through my long career in public service.

Eight years ago, I traveled to France for the 50th Anniversary of the Allied landings in Normandy, France. I went to honor the soldiers—some of them friends—who made the ultimate sacrifice in the name of freedom and to reflect upon the cause to which America and her allies dedicated almost four years. Those ceremonies in France reaffirmed my faith in our cause. I left convinced that our struggles had not been in vain and that our victories made the world a better place.

In our fight to protect freedom, our losses have been great, but our gains have been far greater. In remembrance of our World War II veterans, Congress authorized the construction of a World War II Memorial on the National Mall in Washington, D.C. I believe it will serve as a lasting tribute to the defenders of our nation and the principles on which it was founded—freedom, justice, and honor. If we continue to live by the ideals embodied by our veterans, the future holds unlimited potential.

Ernest "Fritz" Hollings
United States Senator

Senator Hollings, who served in an anti-aircraft artillery unit, was decorated with the Bronze Star for his actions during World War II. At the age of 26, Hollings was elected to the South Carolina House of Representatives. In 1955, he was elected as the youngest governor in the past century. In 1966, he started his career as United States senator, and has been re-elected five times.

GLOSSARY

ack-ack a British term for anti-aircraft fire

air raid siren the wailing sound used to warn civilians that enemy aircraft were approaching and then departing the area

aircraft carrier a huge ship with a flat deck that served as a runway for carrier-based navy planes

Allies the name for the alliance of the United States, Britain, Russia, and other countries

amphibious assault an attack on land that begins in the water, such as D-Day, with ships bringing troops to the shore, where they disembark and attack the enemy land forces

anti-aircraft gun a powerful weapon that was aimed skyward and used to try to shoot down enemy planes

appeasement the policy of giving in to someone in the hopes it will satisfy him of her and prevent further demands from being made

armistice a truce signaling the end of war

armor steel plating on vehicles such as tanks designed to protect them from machine gun fire and other larger-caliber guns

Axis the name for the alliance of Germany, Italy, Japan, and other countries during World War II

barrage balloons a network of balloons and steel cables used above London and Moscow to snare enemy planes that tried to fly over the cities

black market illegal trade in rationed items, usually at very high prices

bomber a plane whose main purpose is to carry a load of bombs to a target, drop the bombs, and return to home base

bunkers protected (often underground) locations usually reinforced with concrete where soldiers or civilians can wait out an attack

casualty someone in a war who has been injured or killed; i.e., removed from action of battle

cavalry a flanking unit of the army that by World War II was mechanized (using gasoline-powered vehicles)

ceiling price the maximum legal price for an item that a store could charge, set by the Office of Price Administration (OPA)

civilian anyone who was not involved in the military

chancellor a political position in certain European countries that is equivalent to a prime minister

collaborator someone who willingly assists the enemy who has invaded

Communists the political party in control of the Soviet Union during the war, led by Stalin

concentration camps Nazi-run camps where political prisoners and Jews were sent to perform heavy labor under cruel conditions

convoy a group of several ships traveling together for mutual protection

death camps Nazi-run camps where mainly Jews were sent, most of them to immediate death in gas chambers

destroyer a ship whose main function is to seek and destroy submarines

dictator a ruler who takes control of a country and does not allow elections and may use force to get rid of any political enemies

draft the process of selection by the government of young men to serve in the armed forces

dragon's teeth the triangular concrete barricades placed along the Siegfried Line in Germany to try to prevent Allied tanks from getting through

Fascist a person whose political goals include expansion and ruling as a dictator

field gear a soldier's equipment on the battlefield, including tools and a blanket roll

fighter a fast plane whose purpose is mainly to attack other planes or provide protection for a formation of bombers

flak exploding artillery shells fired at aircraft

flamethrower a weapon (either hand-held or on a tank) that shot flames using jellied gasoline

flank to go alongside the main force of attack and either distract the enemy or attack from the side of the enemy lines

furlough a short leave from military service, usually for recreational purposes

genocide the mass killing of a group of people based on their culture, race, or religion

ghetto a small enclosed area in a city or town in which wartime Jews were forced to live, with crowded conditions that encouraged disease and hunger

Great Depression the economic slowdown that began in 1929 and lasted until about 1940, just before the United States entered the war

howitzer a large-caliber gun on wheels that is towed into place by a tractor or jeep

incendiary a bomb designed to ignite whatever it lands on, causing destruction from fire rather than explosion

isolationism the United States policy during the 1930s of staying out of world politics

machine gun an automatic weapon that could fire .30 or .50 caliber rounds rapidly

mortar a weapon used to lob shells high into the air, over obstacles and into enemy territory

Nazis members of the German political party in power from 1933 to 1945

OPA Office of Price Administration, in charge of setting policies on rationing and price limits

Operation Barbarossa German name for the invasion of Russia, June 22, 1941

Operation Torch Allied name for the United States invasion of Tunis in North Africa in 1942

points the "currency" of the rationing system; each rationed item had a value in points

rationing governmental limits set on purchasing certain types of items in order to conserve material and prevent panic and hoarding

refugee someone who has left his or her country because of bad conditions or because the person was in danger because of his or her race or religion

round ammunition consisting of the projectile or bullet, and the shell casing containing the powder charge

shell another name for a round, usually of a larger diameter

shrapnel fragments of exploded shells that can kill people and destroy buildings

sortie a term used each time a warplane flies out on a bombing mission

spearhead an army's strong thrust forward into the enemy's front line, often creating a weak spot

Star of David six-pointed yellow star, a symbol of Judaism, that European Jews were forced to wear so they could be easily identified and singled out for cruel treatment

strafing flying low and riddling enemy targets with machine gun bullets

submachine gun a smaller, handheld version of a machine gun

swastika an ancient symbol that became the symbol of the Nazi Party

tank an armored vehicle that rides on its track and is armed with a large-caliber gun (37 mm or above)

tommy gun nickname of one of the common Allied submachine guns

torpedo the primary weapon of a submarine, it sped through the water toward an enemy ship's hull

trench a hand-dug ditch where soldiers can lie low to avoid being seen by the enemy or hit by stray machine gun fire

U-boat name for the German version of a submarine, short for Unterseeboote

V-1, V-2 unmanned rocket-propelled bombs used for the first time by Germany

VE Day a day to celebrate victory in Europe, May 8, 1945

VJ Day a day to celebrate victory in the Pacific, September 2, 1945

v-mail mail written on a special form that is then photographed onto microfilm before being transported to its destination (the U.S. or military post office) and printed on paper and delivered to the addressee

victory garden name for the backyard fruit and vegetable garden that civilians were encouraged to grow.

RESOURCES

Web Sites for Further Exploration

www.arlingtoncemetery.com/contents.htm
The Arlington National Cemetery Web Site
Here you can explore biographies of dozens of World War II heroes, including for example, Admiral John S. McCain. Click on the "biographies" button at the bottom of the page.

www.americasstory.com/cgi-bin/page.cgi /jb/1929-1945
America's Story Web Site from the Library of Congress
This site features some history and photos about the World War II era, especially aimed at kids.

history.acusd.edu/gen/ww2_links.html
University of San Diego's links Web Page

An excellent page of World War II links on all topics, from the home front to the Holocaust.

www.infoukes.com/history/ww2
The InfoUkes Web Page
A Canadian Web site with a detailed history of World War II in the Ukraine, a place that suffered a harsh fate during the war.

motlc.wiesenthal.com/pages
The Simon Wiesenthal Museum of Tolerance Online Multimedia Learning Center
This site has many articles about all aspects of the Holocaust, including descriptions of key people and places throughout Europe.

www.rosietheriveter.org
The Web site of Rosie the Riveter World War II Home Front National Historical Park in California
Some interesting articles and photos about women's contributions to the war effort.

www.cnmi-guide.com/history/ww2
The CNMI Web site (about the Commonwealth of Northern Mariana Islands in the Pacific)
Includes the story of World War II in the Northern Marianas (including Saipan and Tinian).

remember.org
A Cybrary of the Holocaust
The site features much Holocaust-related information.

www.eisenhower.utexas.edu
The Dwight Eisenhower Library and Museum Web Site
Here you can find all kinds of information about the World War II hero and president.

www.fdrlibrary.marist.edu
The Franklin Roosevelt Digital Library and Digital Archives
The country's great wartime president is commemorated here in words and pictures.

*The Web Site of the Women's Royal Voluntary
Service*
Learn all about the contributions of British
women to the war effort.

www.usd230.k12.ks.us/espictt
*Spring Hills Schools in Kansas—Kids' View of
World War II and the 1940s Era*
A neat site by kids dealing with different
aspects of World War II, including memora-
bilia and a timeline of events.

World War II Museums

These are just a handful of museums around the
United States that have exhibits relating to
World War II. Call first for hours and directions.
Check local listings or the Internet to locate more
World War II museums.

American Airpower Heritage Museum

Midland International Airport
9600 Wright Drive
Midland, Texas 79711
(915) 563-1000

*A museum dedicated to the history of aviation, with
exhibits on World War II.*

American Airpower Museum

1300 New Highway
Farmingdale, New York 11735
(631) 293-6398
*This museum features several World War II planes,
including the personal plane of General "Hap"
Arnold.*

Camp Blanding World War II Museum

Camp Blanding
Green Cove Springs
Starke, Florida 32091
(904) 533-3196
*A World War II era camp transformed into a
museum.*

Cradle of Aviation Museum

Mitchel Field
Garden City, New York 11530
(516) 572-0411
*Numerous airplanes, including World War II planes
in a brand-new museum.*

Eldred World War II Museum

201 Main Street
Eldred, Pennsylvania 16731
(814) 225-2220
Memoribilia, maps, and books about the war.

The Holocaust Memorial & Educational Center of Nassau County

Welwyn Preserve
100 Crescent Beach Road
Glen Cove, New York 11542
(516) 571-8040
*This museum features artifacts, displays on holo-
caust survivors, and contemporary art relating to the
Holocaust.*

Museum of Jewish Heritage—A Living Memorial to the Holocaust

Battery Park City
18 First Place
New York, New York 10004
(212) 968-1800

Intrepid Sea-Air-Space Museum

Pier 86
12th Avenue and 46th Street
New York, New York 10036
(212) 245-0072
*A World War II era aircraft carrier is home to
exhibits and carrier planes.*

National D-Day Museum

945 Magazine Street
New Orleans, Louisiana 70130
(504) 527-6012
*A museum devoted to the events of and leading up to
June 6, 1944.*

New Jersey Naval Museum

78 River Street

Hackensack, New Jersey 07601

(201) 342-3268

Among the exhibits are a two-man German coastal defense submarine and a Japanese suicide torpedo.

Palm Springs Air Museum

745 North Gene Autry Trail

Palm Springs, California 92262

(760) 778-6262, x222

A museum featuring World War II aircraft.

Submarine Force Museum

On the water off Thames Street at Crystal Lake
   Road

Groton, Connecticut

(800) 343-0079

Museum featuring the historic submarine Nautilus *and exhibits on submarine history.*

U.S. Air Force Museum

1100 Spatz Street

Wright-Patterson AFB, Ohio 45433

(937) 255-3286

Over 300 aircraft and missiles on display.

USS Missouri Museum

Ford Island

Pearl Harbor, Hawaii

(800) MIGHTYMO

This 887-foot-long (270 m) battleship was the site of the official Japanese surrender in 1945.

United States Holocaust Memorial Museum

1000 Raoul Wallenberg Place, SW

Washington, D.C. 20024

(202) 488-0400

A large museum that includes a permanent exhibition over three floors with more than 900 artifacts and 70 video screens.

Selected Bibliography and Further Reading

(✦ denotes may be suited for children)

✦ Ambrose, Stephen. *The Good Fight: How World War II Was Won.* New York: Atheneum, 2001.

✦ Benford, Timothy. *The World War II Quiz and Fact Book.* New York: Perennial Books, 1982.

Bierman, John. *Righteous Gentile. The Story of Raoul Wallenberg, Missing Hero of the Holocaust.* New York: The Viking Press, 1981.

✦ Boyle, David. *World War II: A Photographic History.* The Netherlands: Metro Books, 2000.

Braham, Randolph L. *The Politics of Genocide in Hungary, Volumes I and II.* New York: Columbia University Press, 1981.

Butcher, Harry C. *My Three Years with Eisenhower: The Personal Diary of Captain Harry C. Butcher, USNR, Naval Aide to General Eisenhower, 1942 to 1945.* New York: Simon and Schuster, 1946.

Churchill, Winston S. *The Second World War.* Boston: Houghton Mifflin Co., 1950.

✦ Considine, Bob. *The Long and Illustrious Career of General Douglas MacArthur.* Greenwich, CT: Gold Medal Books, 1964.

Dunn, George M. *A Diary.* On file at Marine Corps Historical Center in Washington, D.C.

Eisenhower, Dwight D. *Crusade in Europe.* Garden City: Doubleday and Co., Inc., 1948.

Erickson, John. *The Road to Berlin: Stalin's War with Germany.* New Haven, CT: Yale University Press, 1983.

Erickson, John. *The Road to Stalingrad: Stalin's War with Germany.* New Haven, CT: Yale University Press, 1975.

Ethell, Jeffrey L. *Jane's World War II Aircraft*. Glasgow, Scotland: HarperCollins Publishers, 1995.

✛ Frank, Anne. *The Diary of a Young Girl*. New York: Prentice Hall, 1993.

Grove, Eric, and Christopher Chant, David Lyon, Hugh Lyon. *The Military Hardware of World War II*. New York: The Military Press, 1984.

✛ Landau, Elaine. *The Warsaw Ghetto Uprising*. New York: New Discovery Books, 1992.

Leapman, Michael. *Witness to War: Eight True-Life Stories of Nazi Persecution*. New York: Scholastic Inc., 1998.

Marrus, Michael R. *The Holocaust in History*. New York: New American Library, 1987.

✛ Mauldin, Bill. *Up Front*. New York: The World Publishing Company, 1945.

McCombs, Don, and Fred Worth. *World War II Super Facts*. New York: Warner Books, 1983.

Padfield, Peter. *War Beneath the Sea: Submarine Conflict During World War II*. New York: John Wiley and Sons, Inc., 1995.

Physics Manual for Pilots: Flight Preparation Training Series. Published under the supervision of the Training Division, Bureau of Aeronautics, U.S. Navy. New York: McGraw-Hill Book Co., 1943.

✛ Pyle, Ernie. *Brave Men*. New York: Henry Holt and Co., 1944.

Ryan, Cornelius. *The Longest Day*. New York: Crest Books, 1960.

Shirer, William L. *The Rise and Fall of the Third Reich: A History of Nazi Germany*. New York: Simon and Schuster, 1960.

✛ Siegel, Aranka. *Upon the Head of the Goat, A Childhood in Hungary, 1939–1944*. New York: Signet/New American Library, 1983.

Smith, Danny. *Wallenberg: Lost Hero*. New York: Templegate Publishers, 1986.

Sontag, Raymond J. *A Broken World: 1919–1939*. New York: Harper and Row Publishers, 1971.

Swift, Michael, and Michael Sharpe. *Historical Maps of World War II Europe*. London: PRC Publishing Ltd., 2000.

Thalmann, Rita, and Emmanuel Feinermann. *Crystal Night: 9–10 November 1938*. New York: Holocaust Library, 1974.

This Fabulous Century: 1940–1950. New York: Time Life Books, 1988.

Various authors. *Time Life Series on World War II*. New York: Time-Life Books, various dates.

Wicks, Ben. *No Time to Wave Goodbye: The Story of Britain's Wartime Evacuees*. New York: St. Martin's Press, 1988.

Wooldridge, E.T., editor. *Carrier Warfare in the Pacific: An Oral History Collection*. Washington, DC: Smithsonian Institution Press, 1993.

World War II: A Visual Encyclopedia. London: PRC Publishing Ltd., 1999.

Zucotti, Susan. *The Italians and the Holocaust: Persecution, Rescue, Survival*. New York: Basic Books, Inc., 1987.

KEY PERSONALITIES OF WORLD WAR II

Winston Churchill (1874-1965)
Prime Minister of England during the war years, he was seen as a tough bulldog of a leader with a soft spot inside for the British people. His inner strength guided Britain through air raids that killed thousands. His close relationship to President Roosevelt helped the Allies overcome the German threat.

Dwight David Eisenhower (1890-1969)
Five-star general in charge of the D-Day landings and Supreme Commander of the Allied Expeditionary Forces in Europe after the invasion. He was later elected president of the United States. A brilliant strategist and politician, he excelled as a a commander of the Allies.

Emperor Hirohito (1901-1989)
Hereditary leader of Japan throughout World War II. Though not directly responsible for Japan's entry into the war, he refused to surrender until after the atomic bomb was dropped.

Adolf Hitler (1889-1945)
Dictator who ran Germany from 1933 until his suicide in 1945. Hitler quickly rearmed Germany and in 1938 took over Austria and Czechoslovakia. In September 1939, Germany invaded Poland, setting off World War II. During the war, Hitler ordered that the Jews be eliminated from Europe.

Douglas MacArthur (1880-1964)
Charismatic United States general who led the Allies to victory in the Pacific. Though forced to leave the Philippines early in the war, he made a triumphant return in October 1944.

Bernard Montgomery (1887-1976)
British Field Marshall who was Rommel's main opponent in North Africa. Later he was in charge of the D-Day invasion forces on the ground in Europe. He was known for the characteristic beret he always wore.

Benito Mussolini (1883-1945)
Italian dictator from 1922 until September 1943, when the Allies invaded Italy. He conquered Ethiopia in 1935 and Albania in 1939. Hungry for more territory, he became an ally of Hitler. He was captured and hung in 1945.

George S. Patton (1885-1945)
General who led the United States in Northern Africa, then Sicily, and finally the Third Army in its sweep through Europe, beginning in 1944. A brilliant field general whose no-nonsense style helped the Allies make rapid progress.

Erwin Rommel (1891-1944)

German Field Marshal nicknamed the "Desert Fox," he was best known for his excellent field tactics in the deserts of North Africa during the early years of the war. In 1944, he was arrested for being involved in a plot to assassinate Hitler, and forced to kill himself to avoid being shamed in public.

Franklin Delano Roosevelt (1882-1945)

President of the United States from 1933 until his death in office in April 1945. He was elected to an unprecedented four terms, though he only served a few weeks of his fourth term. Roosevelt is credited with successfully guiding the country through the Great Depression and war years, and is judged by historians as one of the top three presidents.

Joseph Stalin (1879-1953)

Dictator who ran the Soviet Union after the death of Lenin. He was an ally of Germany until the Germans invaded Russia in 1941. After the war, Stalin had an uneasy relationship with the United States and Western Europe, having taken control of several European countries, including the eastern half of Germany.

Harry S Truman (1884-1972)

President of the United States after Roosevelt's death in 1945. He had the difficult task of leading the country through the final months of the Pacific war, and made the critical decision to use the atomic bomb on Japan in August 1945.

INDEX